E
L

P

C

The brilliant book of calm

The brilliant book of

Calm

Down to earth ideas for finding inner peace in a chaotic world

Tania Ahsan

brilliantideas

CAREFUL NOW

It takes a special kind of talent to manage to cause yourself harm, injury or loss through reading a book. I couldn't possibly take the credit for that away from anyone. As such the publishers and I accept no responsibility for anything bad that might happen as a result of you reading this book or tripping over it. To be fair, we also don't accept responsibility for anything good that might happen either (the book's publicist just took a sharp intake of breath). Only you can make a book change your life for better or worse. Doesn't that make you feel big and powerful? Yay you!

For Savera, T.T.

Copyright © Infinite Ideas Limited, 2008

The right of Tania Ahsan to be identified as the author of this book has been asserted in accordance with the Copyright, Designs and Patents Act 1988.

First published in 2008 by
Infinite Ideas Limited
36 St Giles
Oxford, OX1 3LD
United Kingdom
www.infideas.com

A CIP catalogue record for this book is available from the British Library

ISBN: 978-1-905940-81-3

Brand and product names are trademarks or registered trademarks of their respective owners.

Designed by Baseline Arts Ltd, Oxford
Typeset by Sparks, Oxford – www.sparkspublishing.com
Printed in India

Brilliant ideas

Brilliant features

Each chapter of this book is designed to provide you with an inspirational idea that you can read quickly and put into practice straight away.

Throughout you'll find three features that will help you get right to the heart of the idea:

- *Here's an idea for you* … Take it on board and give it a go – right here, right now. Get an idea of how well you're doing so far.

- *Defining idea* … Words of wisdom from masters and mistresses of the art, plus some interesting hangers-on.

- *How did it go?* If at first you do succeed, try to hide your amazement. If, on the other hand, you don't, then this is where you'll find a Q and A that highlights common problems and how to get over them.

Introduction

Yoda is my hero. Not because he's a Jedi master or because he ignores the rules of grammar, more because Yoda is an oasis of calm in the face of crisis. When I'm hit by a crisis, I get flappy-handed and shrill; I am pointedly not an oasis of calm, more a cactus of panic. So what qualifies me to write a book on finding inner peace?

Well, in my own search, I've marched confidently up to dead ends and stumbled blindly into unexpected answers. I have been a mind, body, spirit writer and editor for over a decade and I've been an ideas junkie for even longer than that. The nicest thing that someone's ever said to me is that I always seem to be happy and smiling. Clearly that person had had a little too much to drink and couldn't remember the sulks, the pouts and endless, endless complaining but I was grateful for his poor memory nonetheless.

In all my life, I have just encountered two people I think personify inner peace; one is my friend Alex, who seems to be able to deal with any stressful situation with careful planning, an iron will and a list. The other is my friend Simon, who had proper Buddhist monk training in Thailand for several years and so, in my opinion, is actually cheating. The rest of my friends and family are at times calm and serene and, at other times, stressed and shouty. This book is primarily for those of you who wish you were a bit more of the former and a bit less of the latter (except you don't have the time and inclination for years of Buddhist monk training).

Now one of the key things that you'll find in this book, and in a search for inner peace generally, is encouragement to just relax. We're so driven in our society that we think even feelings of calm should be competitive. 'I'm calmer and more sorted than you, na-na-nah-na-nah.' If you don't feel serenity washing over you like a warm chocolate wave every time you put into practice one of these suggestions, please don't start banging your head against the floor, sobbing 'I never get anything right! Even inner peace eludes me, aaaarggghhh!!' Just relax, there's no pass rate and no certificate at the end – though if you want me to make you one, you can send off for one at £89.99 plus postage and packing (I'm kidding, come on, I'm kidding).

Dipping in and out of these ideas, you'll find that a lot of the ideas are things you can do straight away. This is because sometimes it's nice to have dessert first in a meal, even if it does feel slightly indulgent. It seems silly to save the best for last. You won't be made to plough through reams of theory before you get a nugget of practical application; you get to dive right in. If trying the ideas in this book gets you fired, divorced or arrested, please refer to Idea 1 and don't send me poison pen letters. Getting these ideas together has been the result of me quitting a job, getting dumped and getting an unofficial ticking-off from a policeman so I've paid my dues already.

The fact is, inner peace isn't something that comes when you finally paint the whole house a nice shade of cream and start drinking herbal tea. Inner peace is something that is shaped by the wisdom that 'this too shall pass' and is fired in the kiln of self-knowledge (it sounded less pretentious in my head).

Often the times we need inner peace most are the times that we're in turmoil and so don't have time to sit around reading books. However, this is precisely the time to call a halt and do some contemplation. Problems, both serious and trivial, have a way of making us lose the one thing we should always try to keep – perspective. No matter how stressful or miserable life gets, inner peace comes from knowing that you will get through it. There *is* a future life that might bear little relation to your current one.

This book will try to give you some inspiration as to what that future life might look like if you decide to make choices with your inner peace in the forefront of your mind. It is not a book to be read and put away on the shelf to impress visitors (Kafka and Tolstoy are generally better for that sort of thing); it is a workbook of suggestions to put into practice. Though the suggestions won't seem like work so perhaps that should be 'playbook' rather than 'workbook'. Except that sounds a bit infantile. OK, never mind what you call it; in the words of Master Yoda: 'Try it, like it you may'.

1

You're the boss of you

Taking responsibility for your own life may be the toughest thing you do in your quest for inner peace. But the sooner you realise that you're your own knight in shining armour the better.

The President of the United States is the highest office in that country for the same reason that you hold the highest office in your life; the buck stops with you.

The life you lead is the result of decisions that you have made and are constantly making. This is not to say that the outside world doesn't have any influence – of course it does – but ultimately you're running the show. You must not cave in to feeling powerless to make changes in your own life. While you may only have limited control over what you do, you can exercise full control over what you feel and how you react to those limitations.

Here's a typical example: your boss decides to give you a report to do last thing on a Friday night and wants it first thing on Monday morning. It is probably not a practical response for you to jack in your job (though if you have to miss your wedding or a relative's funeral to do it and your boss doesn't cut you some slack, you may do well to start looking at the jobs ads). However, how you deal with a) the feelings this invokes in you and b) the actual task ahead can be vital to your sense of inner peace.

A bad way to respond would be to stomp off home with the work, be in a bad mood all weekend and do it angrily and reluctantly, regularly sighing loudly and bemoaning your fate, while snapping at any poor family member silly enough to pass within a few feet of you.

Here's an idea for you...

Do you know what your income and expenditure is? List all your income in one column and all your outgoings in the next and then create a budget that ensures you're not exceeding your income. It's not boring... well OK, it is a bit boring, but boring is better than the serious distress of insolvency.

A better way would be to accept that you've decided to do the work. And you have, because you didn't resign at the point that you were told about it. So you had the power to leave but you didn't. So, having made a decision to do something, do it well. Put on your favourite music, fix yourself something tasty to snack on while you work and maybe even get your partner to work in the same room so you can have a sense of camaraderie. Take regular breaks but, instead of breaking your flow by going to the TV room, go for a short walk instead or have a boogie round the room.

Society is organised in a very complex way and one of the side effects of this organisation is to make you feel very small and insignificant. If we want to buy a house, most of us have to get a mortgage. To get a mortgage you need a job – a very well-paying job if the house is to be in a nice area. To get the partner you want, you have to be attractive to him or her – be it in looks or behaviour. You have to continue to attract if you want to retain your partner. Let's not even start on the demands of the children. In short, it can very quickly seem as if everyone has got a vested interest in your life – except you. You can feel trapped by all of these social restrictions you put on yourself.

'Man is condemned to be free; because once thrown into the world, he is responsible for everything he does.'
JEAN-PAUL SARTRE, being his ever-cheery but highly-perceptive self. Think not of it as being 'condemned' but more 'blessed'.

Defining idea...

The real revolution happens when you realise that this is your own construct. You have made this. You have decided you want this house or that job. Your choice of partner is determined by you. The way you raise your kids is partly determined by you. As such, if you're feeling unhappy and conflicted by any aspect of your life, YOU can change it. Feel that power coursing through your veins – doesn't it feel fantastic? Now get back out there and go 'Grrrrr!' at the world.

How did it go?

Q **My greatest barrier to inner peace is my long working day. How do I gain more control over my working hours?**

A *I also struggled doing 12-hour days for years before I realised one day that it was unreasonable to push myself like that. So I asked for help and reduced hours. I got it. If you don't ask, muttering under your breath won't necessarily work.*

Q **My husband is really bossy and makes all the decisions from which wine to buy for dinner to where to go on holiday. How do I get more control without conflict?**

A *If you keep bottling up this vague discontent, it will eventually explode in a disproportionate way and cause far more conflict than if you nip it in the bud now. Tell your husband calmly how you feel and ask to have an input into joint decisions.*

Q **My sister and I are partners in business but I'm not happy and want to do something else. I'm scared it will ruin our bond if I leave – should I still do it anyway?**

A *What exactly is making you unhappy? Figure out the specifics before you do anything as it may be something you can change without leaving. If it's that you want to do something else then break it to her with a few suggestions of ways she could run the business without you. If she has your best interests at heart, she'll understand.*

2

Courting chance

Amazing coincidence or a message from the universe? Synchronicities can feel like miracles when they're really bizarre but we can actually trigger them ourselves.

Nervous about the unexplained? Well, don't gulp now, cue the spooky music, and take a walk with me into the twilight zone...

What is a synchronicity? Psychologist and philosopher Carl Gustav Jung described synchronicity as a 'meaningful coincidence'. He believed that certain synchronicities were caused by the human mind tapping into the collective unconscious (sort of a super mind for the whole world throughout all time) and accessing information that is then manifested in the external world. The more aware we become of synchronicities, the better we can understand the behaviour that leads them to happen. So if you dream of a woodpecker and the next day you're woken by a woodpecker at your window, you should check out what the woodpecker symbolises. That symbol, rather than that specific bird at your window, doubtless has a bit of a message for you.

What's really cool about synchronicities is that they feel like you've wandered into the universe's control centre and started playing with all the buttons and switches. This is why those with a religious bent often describe a really cracking synchronicity as a 'miracle'. Whether or not you're religious, what's miraculous is that you can lead synchronicities to happen just by paying attention to them when they do.

Here's my very best one (though health freaks look away now):

My mate Joel and I were stranded in a field in Lancashire once. We were at a festival called Pendle Witch Camp and neither of us had driven there so we couldn't pop down to the nearest town. We'd run out of cigarettes but, because we're both merely social smokers, we couldn't be bothered to find a person to drive us into town. Walking down a country lane, Joel said to me: 'I really fancy some smokes right about now.'

Here's an idea for you...

The next time you see an unusual word in a magazine or book, note it mentally in your head. Then see how many times it comes up in the next week or so. You'll be amazed at how often you find it, in a variety of different places. But it has to be really unusual and a word you're unlikely to come across very often. Unfortunately the first time I noticed this was with the word 'necrophilia' – if you don't know what that is, go look it up, I'm not explaining.

I looked up and there was a packet of cigarettes rammed into the hedge by the side of the road. I walked up to them while Joel said 'Oh, that'll be empty, that will'. Lo and behold, a full packet of cigarettes, abandoned in a hedge at a time that we were walking past going 'I fancy a smoke'. Is that an amazing coincidence or something more?

Joel, who has a peculiarly egalitarian relationship with God, simply said 'would have preferred rolling tobacco but I suppose this'll do'.

How is all this relevant to inner peace? Well, these synchronicities are trying to tell you something. The case of the woodpecker might have been interpreted as the person needing to work harder to get the outcome they want to have happen. A woodpecker, after all, pecks at the wood continuously and has a long tongue to get out the grubs that live under the bark of trees. My own experience with the cigarettes probably wasn't the universe contradicting the Surgeon General's health warning but more a sign that you only have to ask and you shall receive. I was going through a period of extreme mistrust of the universe's abundance then so it definitely perked me up.

'"It's a poor sort of memory that only works backwards," the Queen remarked.'

LEWIS CARROLL's Alice is given some pointers on thinking forwards by the White Queen in *Through the Looking Glass*.

Defining idea…

The search for inner peace gets completely stalled if you become jaded with the world. You have to have a bit of mystery and magic and a good synchronicity provides for that. This doesn't mean that you have to forego all rational thought and start running naked through your garden calling to the pixies; it just means that it's OK to retain a sense of wonder when things happen that are unexplainable by science bods. It doesn't mean you're losing your grip on reality or that the film *The Matrix* was all factual, it just means that you sometimes get a heads-up from the universe. So pay attention.

How did it go?

Q **I had a brilliant synchronicity come up but when I told my partner about it, she mocked it as a straightforward coincidence. How do I convince her?**

A *You don't need to convince her. The fact is that synchronicities are only meaningful insofar as they impact you and your psyche. You're not responsible for making your partner feel all sparkly inside too. In future, if you think your parade is going to be rained on, just don't mention it.*

Q **How do you tell what is a synchronicity and what is a simple coincidence?**

A *Does it give you a wibbly feeling inside? Yes, that scientific term is the one I'm using. Thinking about your Aunt Madge and then running into her down your local supermarket is a coincidence if she lives in your area and a synchronicity if she lives in Australia and you live in Britain. Judge by how much it fills you with a sense of 'Wow!'.*

Q **I've never had a synchronicity happen in my life. Does this mean the universe isn't speaking to me?**

A *Perhaps you're just more sorted than the rest of us and don't need pointers from the universe to instil a sense of wonder or make you pay attention to some aspect of your behaviour. Or you could just not be looking out for them and so, when they happen, they pass you by. Either way, there is no 'synchronicity exam' that you'll have to sit at some point, so relax.*

3

Sell fish

Being selfish isn't the most terrible thing you can be. In fact, if you're a bit of a doormat it may be the best thing you can do for yourself.

Good boys and girls aren't selfish. Good boys and girls have stress-induced heart attacks before the age of 40 or run off and abandon all the responsibilities they've kept up for years once they hit middle age. Be bad.

Imagine that there's a fisherman who sells his catch off the dock. A pretty girl walks by and asks the fisherman if he'll make a present of a fish to her. The fisherman, being a red-blooded straight male, agrees and gives her two for good measure. While he's busy chatting up the girl, a seagull swoops down and nicks two more of his fish before he can stop it. An old man comes by, criticises the state of the fish and asks for a discount of 50%. As the day is getting on now and the fisherman has yet to sell a fish, he agrees to a 50% sale. The man only buys one small fish. The fisherman doesn't have much of his catch left by now but just as he gets ready to holler out his wares, a man with a knife runs up to the dock, threatens the fisherman and steals the rest of his catch. The fisherman is left with nothing but the pathetic 50% sale of a small fish.

Did you like my metaphor there? Tortured, wasn't it? Well, there's a serious point behind it. While we'd like to believe in the abundance of the universe, the fact is that we are temporal creatures, bound to this space–time continuum, and time is a finite commodity in our world. Your quest for inner peace will be seriously derailed if you let time bandits steal away your catch. Whether you overindulge in socialising (the pretty girl), extra unexpected chores (the seagull), family commitments (the old man) or work (the thief), you leave nothing but a tiny pathetic sliver of time for yourself – most of which you'll spend sleeping.

So what can you do about it? Get selfish. This is almost impossible for some as we've been brought up to believe that only very horrible people put themselves before others. Now I'm not suggesting that you leave for a golfing holiday just as your wife goes into labour or that you choose a spa break over a relative's funeral but I do believe that if you don't factor in some time for yourself, you will explode like a pressure cooker. And nobody wants to clear up that sort of mess.

Women are usually the worst for this one as those evil little pod people, sorry, I mean 'children', can make you feel very selfish if their

Here's an idea for you...

Borrow a film that only you want to watch. Hog the TV and DVD player and watch that film that only you want to watch. If your partner or family protest, stick your fingers in your ears and go 'la-la-la-I'm not listening-la-la-la' until they get fed up and leave.

needs don't come first. Naturally when sprogs are babies, you shouldn't leave them with a dirty nappy and no food while you go get your nails done. I hear that sort of thing is frowned upon. But you should definitely come to an arrangement with the gentleman who pro-vided 23 of those chromosomes that make up your little bundle of joy so that you can both enjoy at least one evening a month away from the demands of the petite dictator. And if you can rope a willing relative into looking after Junior so you can both escape together, so much the better.

> **'I am a greedy, selfish bastard. I want the fact that I existed to mean something.'**
> HARRY CHAPIN, the musician and humanitarian philanthropist.

Defining idea...

Adopt a similar policy with regards to housework. Paid work is harder to get selfish about (unless you're the boss and can delegate things) but you can certainly ensure an equitable division of labour at home. But don't be rigid about it. If you love ironing but hate hoovering and your partner loves hoovering but hates ironing, you have the makings of a beautiful partnership. If you both hate doing everything, spend Junior's college fund on a cleaner. It's not selfish, it's sensible.

How did it go? **Q**   **If I stop doing all the things I do for my family, they just won't get done. I don't want to live in a hovel – what's the solution?**

A   *Create your own oasis of calm. Choose a room that you will primarily be in and keep it spotless and perfect, while the rest of the house goes to pot. Eventually your family will realise that they have to pitch in. Or alternatively giant rats will infest the house and eat your family. Either way, problem solved.*

Q   **I've forgotten how to have fun doing things I enjoy – will my pleasures always hinge on other people's?**

A   *Don't worry, I know how you feel; the first time I went off on a break by myself I felt so bored, I felt like going home. But by the third mini-me-break, I was having a fantastic time. You have to retrain yourself to enjoy your pleasures.*

Q   **I did carve out 'me time' this month and went out to dinner with my best friend. My husband accused me of being selfish because it coincided with the night he wanted to invite his mum round. Now both of them are acting like I'm devil spawn; how do I get over that reaction?**

A   *Well done! If you've never been accused of being selfish and one month of doing a couple of things for yourself gets you the accolade of being 'selfish', you've come far, kid. Develop a thick skin. You don't have to always put yourself first but when you do, don't let anyone bully you out of it.*

4

Beam me up

Smiling is probably the simplest way to win friends and influence people and yet we use it so sparingly, we've almost forgotten the art of a beaming delivery.

Light up a room with your smile and you'll be seen as instantly likeable and approachable — unless you have a particularly sinister-looking grin.

One of the first things we'll ever do that gets us love and admiration is smile. Of course if we have particularly negative parents, they'll assure everyone that it's just gas and steal some of the shine away from our very first winning performance.

Humans are basically big apes and we love looking at each other. We connect via the eyes and then we decide in a split second if we like someone by the features on their face and also whether that face looks friendly or not. Now it's not necessarily the case that smiling away like the village idiot is going to get you much game. For example, many women I know (and myself for that matter) tend to go for Byronic, moody men who would rather swallow razors than give someone a toothy grin. There's a good reason for this as researchers have found that men with high testosterone (the uggh male hormone) levels are less smiley. So we are capable of finding

Here's an idea for you...

Smile at everyone you meet today. You don't have to put Vaseline on your teeth or anything, just make some eye contact and give a brief smile to everyone you encounter, stranger and friend alike. Don't do it self-consciously and don't descend into doom if people don't return your smile.

You'll find that you get a warm, fuzzy feeling almost immediately. If it makes you feel uncomfortable, like you're coming onto everyone you meet, then start small by smiling at babies and animals. That's universally acceptable to just about everyone (except those who regularly read the tabloids and have naturally suspicious minds as a result).

unsmiling folk attractive but I would argue that sullen sultriness doesn't really win you many friends.

I have to admit at this point that I have a bit of a problem in this department. When I'm lost in thought, I look like I'm in a real strop or, at the very least, incredibly aloof. Occasionally I may even look like I'm going to brain someone when all I'm thinking about is what to have for tea. If you have a face that looks a bit aggressive and angry, even when you're not feeling that at all, it can be a real affliction. You have to consciously remember to smile even more than normal folk. However, most of you out there won't suffer from this problem so you have no excuse.

A smile is one of the few things that is universally recognised as an expression of happiness. Someone with too much funding for fairly useless research found that we use 18 distinct types of smile in a variety of different social situations. However, the two you'll be most familiar with are the real smile and fake one. A fake one rests on the mouth and doesn't make it as far as the eyes but a proper smile crinkles the corners of your eyes and just 'feels' genuine. While you should be aiming for real smiles, Stepford ones will do until you get there as you can 'trick' your body into thinking you're happy by acting as if you are.

'At some point, I realised something was wrong with my face. It was smiling.'
CHARLIE BROOKER, humorist and *Guardian* columnist, finds something of merit in his uncomfortable trip to the Glastonbury festival.

Defining idea…

Endorphins (those cute little biochemical compounds) are released when you laugh or smile and they work much the same way as opiates so if your dealer is on holiday, sorry, I mean if you want a natural sense of well-being and joy, get grinning. Rent out a funny film if you're out of practice in smiling or play with your kids – I hear they say the funniest things. In short, make smiling a priority in your life.

Write it into your filofax if it makes you feel better. Scheduling in some time to smile at the world as it goes by is one of the best exercises you can do for your soul. And if you keep being accused of being miserable, stop everything until you can manage to raise a genuine smirk. Nobody likes being thought of as a grumpy grouch, unless of course you're a gorgeous male model who makes his money from frowning semi-naked in photos. Phwoar.

How did it go?

Q **I smiled at everyone and got asked out by a really unfortunate-looking man. What have you started?!?**

A *Well, a danger of being more attractive to the world is that the world isn't always as attractive as you'd want it to be. Persevere as you're not doing this to attract blokes but to feel happier within yourself and no amount of minging men can take that away from you.*

Q **I keep forgetting to smile. How do I remember?**

A *So do I! I'm lost in my own world and, before you know it, I've been accused of being a moody mare. The best thing to do is relax, when you remember, do it, if you don't remember, don't beat yourself up about it. The point of all this smiling is to make you happier not to force you to act unnaturally.*

Q **My baby is quite old now but she still hasn't smiled at anyone. Should I be worried?**

A *Nope. My little sister was the most grumpy baby in the world for months and months after she was born. That's why I believe in reincarnation as she looked like an old man fed up at being reborn yet again. Smiling is universal and eventually your baby will come round to the benefits of turning up the corners of her mouth.*

5
Listen up

Giving people your undivided attention means you start to understand more about the folk around you and those same people are more willing to listen to you too.

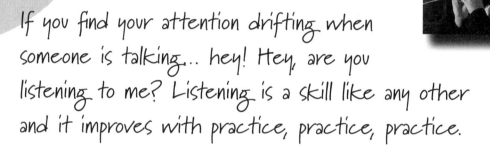

If you find your attention drifting when someone is talking... hey! Hey, are you listening to me? Listening is a skill like any other and it improves with practice, practice, practice.

One of the best compliments I've ever received was from my cousin who said I listened really intensely, like I was really, deeply interested in what the other person had to say. Unfortunately I messed up the compliment by admitting that I only really glared at someone and listened really, really carefully because I have a short attention span and, if I don't do that, I won't take anything in. But, in my defence, at least I noticed that I don't listen to people and have tried to do something about it.

Here's an idea for you...

Listen to one of your favourite songs and write down the lyrics on a piece of paper. Then go to a lyrics website and see what the lyrics actually are. You'll be surprised at the discrepancy. For many, many years I thought the Bananarama lyric 'Robert de Niro's waiting, talking Italian' was 'Talking to me or Tania'. I thought it was great that a song mentioned my name and it was only when a friend of mine heard me singing along to it on the radio that he corrected me and my whole perception of the song changed. Which are your misheard lyrics? And if you're mishearing lyrics then how much more are you mishearing in everyday life?

One of the biggest stumbling blocks to inner peace you'll ever find is the inability of people to listen to each other. Even when folks are listening to each other, they are often applying what I call 'offence filters'. This is whereby everything you say is filtered through to check if it is something to get offended or upset about. This means that the listening is slanted and is not really proper listening at all. I can speak about this with some authority because I am terrible at romantic relationships and this form of listening is one of the key things that contributes to bad relationships. It goes something like this:

Him: 'Why don't we have something a bit healthier for dinner tonight?'

Me: 'You think I'm unhealthy?'

Him: 'No more so than me. That's why a healthy meal would be good for a change.'

Me: 'So you're saying I'm fat and I'm trying to saturate your arteries with my cooking too? Is that it? Well, cheers very much.'

Him: 'I'm going to shut up and sulk now, if it's all the same to you.'

Me: 'No, you're meant to say "I don't think you're fat and your cooking is great". Why do you always get your end of the conversation wrong?'

There it is. You see, bad listening is to do with scripting what the other person is saying before they've said it. It's just waiting for your turn to speak, without really registering what the other person is saying. That's no way to hold a conversation or to show that you care about somebody else.

'Everything has been said before, but since nobody listens we have to keep going back and beginning all over again.'
ANDRE GIDE, author, humanist and Nobel Laureate

Defining idea…

It is an absolute basic of respect for someone else that you listen to him or her. If they then continue talking and talking at you without needing your input at all then you have a valid reason to stop listening (well, except if they're a speaker at a talk as that's sort of the whole point). However, unless they show you that discourtesy, you should give them the benefit of the doubt and listen carefully, with 100% of your attention, to what is coming out of their mouth. You never know, it may be something you've been longing to hear.

How did it go?

Q **I try very hard to listen but I find myself interrupting as I'm scared I'll forget what I was going to say – how do I stop that?**

A *I'm exactly the same. The first thing to do is realise that you're not in a debating society so you don't need to 'score points'. Secondly, slow down. If you listen to someone, ponder what they say and then make your response; you'll find you put your point across much better. Plus they're not about to say what they want and then run away before you can answer. That would be childish. But funny, though.*

Q **My wife always tries to talk to me when I'm doing something else. How can I stop her doing that?**

A *Say 'I'm doing this right now but I'll listen to you as soon as I'm done.' If she insists that her conversation is more important than what you're doing, have a think about it. Are you watching commercials avidly because you've been hypnotised by the TV or are you watching commercials avidly because you work in advertising and need to know something for tomorrow's meeting? If the first, she may have a point; if the second, explain why it's important. Of course by the time you've done that, the commercials will be over and your wife will be sulking and you'll be enraged. But at least you'll have had a conversation about it so that it doesn't happen again.*

Q   My children talk over each other and they seem to think that whoever is loudest will get my attention. How do I stop the madness?

A   *A talking stick. Children (and adults) love the idea of rules and order and if you put the rule that only the person with the talking stick (or bowl or whatever else you don't mind getting broken through excessive passing around) gets to speak, then everyone should theoretically get a turn to speak.*

6

Hugging trees

Nature nurtures if you let it. It's sometimes just a case of tuning in your ears to hearing what that tree, rock or hill is saying to you. Don't worry, it's hardly ever obscene.

If communing with nature makes you think of traumatic camping trips where nature, in the form of beetles, tried to go up your nose, then you need to start letting go of that fear.

My breathing was shallow, I had a pain in my chest and I felt as though my head was going to explode. I really felt like I was dying but I knew I wasn't. I was having a panic attack. I used to have them as a child when we lived in a particularly rough part of London and I hated walking out the front door, such was my sensitivity to the violence I felt was waiting for me outside.

But this time I wasn't a kid any more, I was an editor for a very large company and I was pulling 12-hour days and dealing with a very stroppy boss. Never one to shy away from a fight, I had spent weeks battling my corner in meetings, working all the hours I was awake and not eating or sleeping very well. It was a Sunday and I had just finished one article and was about to start copy-editing another when I had the panic attack. I could feel the tears welling up; I had to get out.

Here's an idea for you…

Go and blow your breath on all the plants in your house. However silly you feel doing it, you're quite happy to breathe in the oxygen that your plants provide so why not give them a little extra gift of carbon dioxide as a sweetener for all their good work? This is especially useful for growing seedlings as they seem to like that sort of thing.

I walked to the Grand Union canal, which runs near my home. I went down to the towpath, under smelly, graffiti-covered bridges, past Sainsbury's and past all the fishermen on the side of the canal. I kept walking and walking, further and further along the towpath. The sunlight made the water sparkle. The odd canal boat chugging along was the only company I had and then I spotted a magical sight: a heron was perched still as stone on the far bank of the canal. I stopped to look at it and when I turned back to the path, I noticed an opening in the hedge to my left. I went through it, up a slight bank and saw that I was in the middle of a field. I can't begin to tell you how weird that was as I live in Wembley, not usually known for its random fields in the middle of nowhere.

In the centre of the field was a huge oak tree. I walked up to the tree and placed my hand against it. I could feel a warmth emanating from the bark into my hands. I immediately felt calmer and more in control. My breathing steadied and everything seemed to grind to a halt. Time stood still and I don't know how long I was there, with my palm against my oaky friend. Eventually I sat for an hour or so with my back against the tree and, when I returned home, I was completely relaxed. It was like having a conversation with a wise, reassuring friend. I revisit that oak whenever I feel like things are getting on top of me and my natural mate never fails to give me solace.

Another really fascinating and relaxing way I interact with plants is to play Linda Long's music CDs. Dr Long is a biochemist and musician and she used her knowledge of the molecular structure of plant proteins to attribute notes to each protein and so created the 'music' of herbs and medicinal plants like pokeweed, white mustard, parsley and clover. It's some of the most chilled, evocative music I've ever heard. She has registered the term Molecular Music for this great experiment in hearing plant life-forms but I just call it nature nurturing.

'A weed is no more than a flower in disguise.'
JAMES RUSSELL LOWELL, poet and abolitionist

Defining idea…

25

How did it go?

Q **I don't have any natural areas around me as I live in the middle of a city. How can I commune with nature if it isn't there?**

A *I'm also a city girl so I can sympathise. However, we should both take a leaf (pardon the pun) out of the book of inner city schools. They get school-children to grow watercress and sunflowers from seed and so can we. Start with fairly easy things like watercress and then start looking at allotments in your area or maybe a window box. Before you know it, you'll have created an oasis of green calm in the midst of your urbanite jungle.*

Q **I'm allergic to pollen and can't go out into nature much. How can I bring nature into my life?**

A *Apart from using one of the good allergy medications that are out there (after advice from your doctor, of course), how about taking comfort from images of nature rather than the real thing? I have a fantastic silver birch screen saver on my computer and pebbles and shells I have collected on various beaches on my desk. All of these are ways to bring the beauty of nature into your life, without a single sneeze.*

Q **I am the kiss of death to all plants. What am I doing wrong?**

A *I'm not naturally green-fingered either. Try keeping low maintenance plants like ferns or aloe vera. If that doesn't work, you may want to try having cut flowers in your home instead as they're a bit like mummies, dead already but still looking mighty fine.*

7

Comfort above all

**Forget Trinny and Susannah, give your poor body a
break from tight clothes and painful shoes. Your body is
quite capable of telling you what not to wear.**

Fashion has absolutely nothing to do with
style. Fashion is an industry, style is an art
form. Fashion will have you running to the shops
every other month; style is eternal.

For me shopping for clothes is definitely one of the circles of hell and I'm surprised
that Dante left it out. I hate it with a deep and abiding passion. I even hated it when
I was the perfect size 10 as I never had a clue what to wear or what was trendy or
looked nice on me. All clothes were hit or miss. Sometimes I looked terrific. Other
times I looked ghastly.

As I got older, things went from bad to worse. I put on masses of weight till I hit my
present fabulously indulgent size 18. Now, not only did I not know what to shop
for, I had to ensure clothes suited my new bigger size. This was not as easy as simply
avoiding hot pants in a size 18. It required a huge amount of figuring out what cuts,
cloths and colours suited me. For someone who hates shopping, I had found a new
level of torment.

Here's an idea for you... **Have a clothes swap party among your friends. Invite everyone round to your house, asking them to bring clothes, shoes and accessories that they no longer want. Clear your own wardrobe too and then pile everything together in the centre of the room and let everyone rummage. Provide some cocktails and nibbles to make it all even more fun and definitely try things on.**

Then I had an epiphany. I was going on a date and so I wore a tight girdle to hold everything in, a young tight, funky top, some capri pants and high heels. I was going for a retro look and I sort of pulled it off but I was in loads of pain. The girdle hurt, the top made me self-conscious about my cleavage and the high heels were killing me. I was no mood to be on a date and I'm sure I was not exactly scintillating company.

As I hobbled home that evening, I had a Scarlet O'Hara moment: I would never be uncomfortable again. That night I called my cousin in Pakistan and instructed her to make me five loose kaftan style tops in silk in a variety of colours. I then went shopping the next day for loose trousers and flat loafers, Mary Janes and flat boots. It was a military-style operation; I didn't allow myself to coo over the heels or to stray into the corsetry department. I wanted comfort. It could be smart and it could be beautiful but it had to be comfortable.

This was because I had learnt a secret. You can only be stylish and elegant when you are feeling comfortable. Most of the gorgeous girls I'd met who were real fashion victims also looked really unhappy most of the time as they were in physical pain from what they were wearing. Pain makes you grumpy. Think of truly stylish women like Audrey Hepburn or Isabella Rossellini and you rarely think of discomfort, more ease of movement, grace. So take a tip from these icons and keep it simple and comfy.

'Fashion is a form of ugliness so intolerable that we have to alter it every six months.'
OSCAR WILDE

Defining idea...

If you're scared you'll end up looking frumpy, remember the magical power of accessories and add funky belts, scarves and jewellery to keep it modern and add interest. Vintage and retro is massively popular now (although I was doing it back when it wasn't and so naturally feel a bit huffy as I was being teased as a teenager for being two decades before my time). The benefit to this trend is that you can dress like your gran and still look cool. What are grannies known for? Great set hairstyles, a good red lipstick and comfy, warm, feminine clothes. It's a winning combination.

The other important point to bear in mind is the use of natural materials, silks and cottons, for example. This is because synthetics can be itchy, lose shape more quickly and just don't feel as nice on the skin. I was also once told by a very spiritual man that silk is like a coat of armour against negativity. Try wearing a silk vest under your clothes for difficult meetings or when you suspect you might encounter conflict and see if it works.

How did it go?

Q **What have comfortable clothes got to do with inner peace?**

A *Back in the day, fakirs and spiritual aspirants would put themselves through extreme discomfort to mortify the flesh and remind them of their spiritual nature. Luckily we don't need to go down that path as evidenced by the number of Thai fishermen pants you see in the average meditation class. Discomfort is old skool spirituality; we're hip and modern here.*

Q **I look like a shapeless blob in the sort of clothes you suggest. What do I do to still look alluring?**

A *For a start stop referring to yourself as a 'shapeless blob'. Try definition. If you can afford tailored trousers, think of the wide legged trousers worn by women in the 1930s and 1940s. They were comfortable but defined too. If you can't afford tailored clothing, head for some of the vintage shops popping up in all major cities and have a good rummage till you find the perfect fit for you. 70s hostess dresses are also very sexy but loose-fitting. Then all you need is a martini and you can re-enact* Abigail's Party *round at yours.*

Q **I love fashion. Are you suggesting I forsake my hobby?**

A *Heck, no! You should embrace your hobby but now you have a mission along with it, find the most wearable and comfortable cuts and styles each season. You'll find certain designers like Miyake and Wakeley kinder on the female form than the McQueens and Gaultiers of the world.*

8

Bomb? What bomb?

Regular news fasts will help you feel better about yourself and other people. Mainly because you won't be wondering if they're a killer and you're about to become their next victim.

There is a reason why ignorance is bliss. Pick up any newspaper you like and you'll soon find out why. Crime and crises are rarely bedfellows to bliss.

This morning the papers were splashed with headlines about a man who was beaten to death. Then there was the young woman killed by her in-laws. Then a scandal regarding people who lost everything in a home development scam and now face retirement in complete poverty. Cheery, isn't it?

Now I'm not belittling, or denying, the fact that terrible things happen in the world. Our newspapers and TVs don't let us forget that for an instant but what would happen if we were forced to hear good news all the time? I'll tell you what;

our blood pressures would be lower, our moods would be happier and we'd have that weird contortion of the face called a 'smile' playing on our lips rather more often.

The author and TV documentary maker, Michael Moore, analysed news coverage in the States and compared it to news coverage in Canada. He believes that more news coverage of violence in the States leads that country to think itself unsafe while a more balanced approach to news in Canada left it feeling quite upbeat about the problem of crime, so much so that in some parts of the country, people still leave their back doors unlocked.

Here's an idea for you...

Ask all your friends and family to look out for bits of good or funny news for you. Nothing horrible or bizarre (unless it evokes a feeling of wonder) but genuinely wonderful news, often hidden away in regional or trade papers or in the news 'nibs' columns. Get them to clip them for you and paste them into a scrapbook of 'good news'. Whenever awful news makes you feel sad or angry, browse your scrapbook.

Back when I was a teenager, I became obsessed with good health and I started devouring alternative health books. My favourite was *8 Weeks to Optimum Health* by Dr Andrew Weil, M.D. In it the good doc laid out his plan for getting to the best of health. This is where I heard about 'news fasts'. He advised that everyone take a day a week when they did not listen to radio news, TV news or pick up a paper. You should start with a day a week and expand it until you mostly don't hear the news.

Now this was the most revolutionary thing I had ever heard. As a journalist, I live and breathe on news. It was like being told to stop breathing. I enlisted my father – also a journalist – for support and we both tried it for a month. The days we news fasted, it was like having missing limb syndrome. You'd go to turn the radio on automatically in the morning and then have to slap your hand away. The same with midday news on the telly.

> *'Nothing travels faster than light, with the possible exception of bad news, which follows its own rules'*
> DOUGLAS ADAMS, author and humorist

Defining idea...

The result? We had one of the happiest months in years. Of course, I'm sure I'll discover that some minor celebrity from my youth is now dead and I don't know it because it fell on my news fast day but what's the worst that could happen? I'll lose out on a pub quiz. So what? The point is I also missed all the train crashes, the cruelty, the stupidity, the near-sighted self-interests of corporations etc., etc. And I am much the happier for it.

If anything really huge happens, trust me, someone will tell you. Bizarrely, when 9/11 happened I was judging a curry competition in Bournemouth. After the competition, a few of us were having a drink in an outdoor café looking out over a gorgeous blue sea. My sister phoned me with the news and said 'go find a TV screen, I can't even explain'. I walked into the café and everyone was stood watching the news like it was the end of the world. And in many ways, it was. The sea was still beautiful but my enjoyment of it was gone. Don't let the news steal any more moments of joy from you.

How did it go? **Q** **I can't stand it any more – I need to know what's happening in the world! I feel dumb at dinner parties. Surely there must be a better way to inner peace?**

A *Do you really feel dumb because you don't know which politician has been having an affair with which celebrity? Or do you just feel left out because all your friends are still caught in the news trap? Better to be trapped with company than free alone – is that it? Well, how about you bring your friends along with you. Tell them what you're doing. Explain why you think the news is so stressful and start that debate at that dinner party.*

Q **My sister calls me up and tells me the news when we're having a conversation so I can't escape it at all. How can I stop her?**

A *Bring the conversation back to her own life. People love talking about themselves and you can distract her from salacious bits of newsworthy gossip by asking her about her own gossip.*

Q **I work in an industry where it's my job to scan the news. How can I avoid it when it's my job?**

A *It sounds dramatic but, depending on how much you love your current job and how stressed you are, perhaps you should get a new job? I think the police, lawyers and judges often concentrate on the letter of the law to avoid looking too closely at the crime itself, as when you're dealing with that daily, you're bound to get very depressed and exhausted. Perhaps a sabbatical is called for?*

9

Shallow grave

How being buried alive can leave you feeling calm and rested. No, really, it can. Obviously not if a serial killer is the one doing the burying but we recommend you use a shaman.

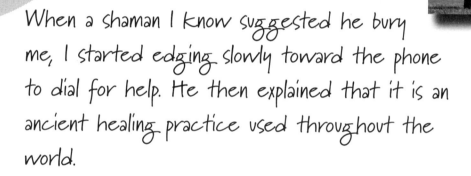

When a shaman I know suggested he bury me, I started edging slowly toward the phone to dial for help. He then explained that it is an ancient healing practice used throughout the world.

Ross Heaven is one of my favourite people in the world. He is also a shamanic healer. In a shamanic healing, you lie down and the shaman 'journeys' for you into the spirit worlds to recover lost parts of you or to get information on how to best heal you. Generally speaking, there's incense being burned and the shaman may drum, use a rattle and will occasionally blow smoke over you to 'cleanse' your spirit and your aura. Shamanism is something I'm quite familiar with because my father

Here's an idea for you...

Get tucked in for a bit. Ask a family member to tuck in your duvet around your bed so you're tightly in there and try relaxing in that position, in the dark, for a time. Only do it for as long as you feel comfortable. You could also play some calming sounds like ocean waves while you're doing this.

has been a practitioner of it for several decades too, but burial was a new one on me.

Apparently the earth 'holds' you and all your problems, negativity and illnesses are absorbed into the earth and taken from you. Since the earth is huge, it can take an awful lot of toxins and process them so that they're not harmful to anyone. The theory all sounded very good but get the practicalities: I would be buried overnight in the earth in the woods and would emerge at dawn the next day. Plus I'd have to dig my own grave. Sounds like a plot from a bad B horror movie, doesn't it?

The woods were rather remote and quiet. Disturbingly, the caretaker for those woods had warned Ross that badgers in the woods become quite aggressive when they're out hunting for worms and grubs so to be wary of approaching one if you see it. Great, not only was I being buried alive, I may get mauled by an irate badger – the day was getting better and better.

You have to fast from midnight the night before you're getting buried. You can have water and the occasional coffee but no food. This makes your body energy lighter and you can better 'tune in' to your healing. From about lunchtime, I had to start digging my grave. I first lay down on the ground and Ross marked with a spade around my body to create a snug, close-fitting shape in the ground. When I stood up, I felt strangely sad at seeing my form marked out on the ground. It was so small and insignificant and, when we die, our bodies are these small, insignificant things we leave behind and yet we give them so much importance while we're alive.

'Forget not that the earth delights to feel your bare feet and the winds long to play with your hair.'

KAHLIL GIBRAN, poet and philosopher

Defining idea...

The digging was awful. My hands got blistered, the ground was rock hard and my back was killing me. If I ever murder someone, the body is not being buried as even a shallow grave takes all day and vast amounts of energy to dig.

Eventually at about 7pm, I got in my 'grave'. I was in a sleeping bag and had planks of wood over the grave to hold the weight of the soil. A big sheet of tarpaulin went over those with a gap at the top so I could breathe. Then the soil went back on top. It was very cosy and I could smell the damp, cold earth around my head. As it got darker, the gap at the top of the tarpaulin became invisible.

I won't lie to you. It was scary as all hell, I thought I could hear madmen with axes approaching to kill Ross (who stays up all night awake next to the person who is being buried, singing and drumming occasionally) and then fill in my grave. I only lasted till just a little after midnight then I yelled to come out. Once out, I had to visualise that I was leaving all my concerns and troubles in the grave and I shovelled the earth back in. When I got back that night, I had a shower and couldn't stop crying. That night I slept really fitfully and in the morning, I felt like a million dollars. A resurrected million dollars.

How did it go?

Q   **The idea of burial is horrible to me as I'm claustrophobic. Any suggestions?**

A   *I'm also claustrophobic and, when I was buried, I only realised how heavy the soil was when I couldn't move my hand to scratch my nose. I started panicking but then deep breaths calmed me down. Be gentle with yourself and don't force a situation if it will make you feel uncomfortable. Try just burying your feet in a sandy beach and imagining all the worries and negativity draining out from your feet and being absorbed and neutralised by the sandy earth.*

Q   **Burial is too extreme for me but I am interested in finding out more about shamanic healing. Any ideas?**

A   *Try contacting The Four Gates Foundation (www.thefourgates.com) for courses in shamanism and for individual shamanic healing.*

Q   **My husband says I've become a New Age hippy with all these 'alternative' practices. How do I get him and my family to take me seriously?**

A   *If you don't rise to the jibes, they'll stop teasing you. They probably only do it now because they know that it bothers you. Alternatively, you could sit them down and tell them how upset you get when they tease you. Except if your family is anything like mine, that'll just be more fodder for them!*

10

Far out, man

You can achieve an altered state without needing to find your nearest drug dealer – honestly, you can. You just need to start engaging with the world again.

If you're stuck in a rut, it can feel as though nothing is new or special. When that feeling of stagnation hits you, you need to find ways to achieve a new state of being.

Meditation doesn't work for me. Being a mind, body and spirit editor that's a bit of shameful admission as we're all supposed to be meditation adepts who can hightail it to a higher state of awareness quicker than you can say 'Ooooommmmmmm'. But altered states can be achieved in ways other than sitting around in pristine white clothes chanting with our eyes closed.

For example, I don't need pot. I have a friend called Nish who has the exact same effects as those that potheads crave. She makes you feel relaxed and the longer you

Here's an idea for you... **Try spinning around in the garden, like you used to when you were little and then when you stop, lie down on the grass and look at the sky. This gives you a sensation like the earth is moving beneath you. Well, it certainly moved for me anyway.**

spend in her company, the more you're likely to start giggling. She also makes you not want to get up and leave to start your day. You just want to stay there and get high on her. However, she has none of the side effects. You're unlikely to receive a police caution (well, at least as long as she's not driving). You're also unlikely to be sold Nish cut with bad things that will make you ill. Nish is the perfect recreational drug.

Do you have anyone like that in your life? Someone who is so engaged with everything and so interested in you that they make you think that, hey, perhaps I am interesting after all! If you don't, you need to begin a quest to find someone like that. Perhaps you had someone like that but you lost touch? If so, find them again.

For others, music is the path to a drug-free high. I have had more spiritual moments listening to the Counting Crows than I have meditating. I know some folks who devote vast tracts of time, money and energy to music. They're not musicians but they've found a way to reach a state of joy and engagement through appreciating the music made by others.

Engagement is the word you're looking for. Not the big diamond ring kind but the 'can't take my eyes off this' kind. Now, here's an exercise. Close your eyes. Take three deep breaths. Don't worry, I'm not going to ask you to mediate. You can open your eyes again. Now, think really hard of where and when you last felt completely joyous. Properly joyous. It could be when you last laughed so hard, you cried. Or it could be something more wacky.

'He does not need opium. He has the gift of reverie.'
ANAIS NIN, diarist and author

Defining idea…

My personal one is from last Christmas when I got invited as a 'plus one' to someone's office Christmas party. I'm not a corporate person so the thought of an evening making small talk with people I didn't know wasn't filling me with hope and excitement. However, I wanted to see the friend who had invited me and I figured we could chat the night away, even if it was a bit of a chore to be with others. The party was a surprise one as no-one had been told where we were being taken. A bunch of cabs had been booked to take all the guests to a secret location.

When we got there, the place was just a black door with a doorman outside. It was in middle of somewhere random like Kennington. Once we stepped through the door though, it was completely different. We were in an enchanted garden, all themed in a 'horror' style with dry ice acting as fog and moving mechanical creatures in the garden. Through the garden was Simon Drake's House of Magic! There followed the best evening of magic and cabaret I have ever seen and it created a memory like no other. I felt like I was five again and seeing the world anew. That sense of wonder is what you should be aiming for.

How did it go?

Q **My son says that he finds German death metal music relaxing. Is he having me on?**

A *Probably not. I used to find Alice Cooper relaxing as a teenager and there was one summer that my parents refused to come into my room because of my collection of glam metal rocker posters. It meant I had an even more relaxing summer, so your son is probably relaxing in earnest.*

Q **I can't remember a time I felt engaged. I feel like I've always felt this 'blah' about everything. What should I do?**

A *Pretend. One of the best ways to kick yourself out of a rut is to act as if you're having a fantastic time doing something new, even if you're not. Take a life drawing class, go pay a visit to friends you haven't seen in a while, buy a new CD. Slowly you'll find that while you were pretending to be loving it, you started actually loving it.*

Q **I feel like I'm in a completely altered state when I sculpt but my brother, who's an art dealer, says my pieces aren't very good and now I feel like giving up. Should I?**

A *Come on now, you know what I'm going to say to that, don't you? Of course you shouldn't give up! Your brother is the worst person to judge whether your work is any good. He knew you when you had a snotty nose and can't really place you in his imagination as an artist. He's also concerned with the commercial business of selling art which has very little to do with real art. The tales of artists discovered to be great only after their deaths are too numerous to list here.*

11

Retox for life

Bring on the booze and fags – you know you want to. Try this weekend retox and see whether a lot of what you fancy does you any good.

Frightening health reports have us regarding our food and drink with suspicion. You never know what is going to be found to be lethal for us next.

Everything is terrible for you. Meat? Awful. Dairy products? Forget it. White bread? Bad idea. Actually, all wheat comes to your bread bin via Satan's inner sanctum. It is baked in the fires of hell and is there simply to cause you to put on weight and then have a heart attack before your time. Vitamins aren't that great for you either because you never know what the capsules they're contained in are made of. And you could be overdoing them anyway.

No, the best thing for you to do is not eat. Or drink. Except pure water triple-filtered and served at room temperature. Aaargggh! When did we become so LA? Not wanting to offend readers in LA but I personally love going there just to eat juicy, succulent steaks and thick cut fries. Simply because it's considered on a par with mugging pensioners in that crazy city. You can always tell the tourist or the out-of-towner there as they'll be the ones with bad teeth who actually eat, rather than

Here's an idea for you... **Go for a traditional cream tea or to an ice cream parlour and enjoy a big treat. If you can't afford that, make your own sundae at home. Ensure you get as many toppings as possible and relish every bite. You are banned from making comments like 'the diet starts tomorrow' or 'this'll go straight to my hips'.**

push food around their plates, as if they were examining particularly revolting slugs.

People, this is no way to live. I know, I've been there. I've tried every diet and healthy eating plan under the sun. You name it, I've denied myself it. It got so I couldn't actually see what was being offered to me, all I could see was calorific content. It didn't matter if my taste buds zinged at the idea of eating what was put in front of me, I had to first ascertain if it was 'safe' for me to eat. I no longer enjoyed food. It was all just a mathematical equation and not particularly exciting math either.

One day I popped out to the supermarket to get some lunch and I returned an hour later, on the verge of tears. I had been unable to decide on my lunch as I had picked up one sandwich after another, calculating the calorie value and then putting it down again. I was so determined to pick a meal that was healthy and non-fattening that I had no idea what I was doing. I didn't pick up anything because it looked appealing but only because it looked low fat.

I stopped dieting and started remembering what I really enjoyed eating. I love Cornish ice cream, meringues, carrot cake, seafood, medium-rare steak with new potatoes, Yorkshire puddings, rocket and parmesan salad with balsamic vinegar, cheeses, pasties, oooooh chocolate, and sushi. I began a litany of all my favourite foods, some of which were good for me and some of which weren't. Then that weekend, I had a massive feast with several of the dishes I named there for me. I didn't just wolf them down. I ate with all my senses. Before I get all Nigella on you, it was a sensuous delight. Best of all, I didn't once think 'I wonder what the calorie content of that is?'

We tend to save treats for special occasions like Christmas or birthdays but have some champagne this weekend to start off your retox and then maybe make yourself some canapés to have before supper. Yes, it's indulgent (especially if you're dining alone) but you deserve a treat as much as those guests you would normally slave over a hot stove for. By the end of the weekend, you'll have restored your sense of serenity through mindful eating of all that gives you 'happy mouth'.

'When choosing between two evils, I always like to pick the one I never tried before.'
MAE WEST, actress and supreme Queen of wit

Defining idea...

How did it go?

Q   **I can't possibly do as you're suggesting. I'll become overweight and miserable! What kind of advice is this?**

A   *Aha! So it's true then. You don't trust yourself. You assume that spending one weekend eating and drinking and doing exactly what you want will result in a whole lifetime of debauchery and excess? Relax, you're not some dangerous animal who's going to eat all the pies. Give yourself a break and try to bring that relaxation into your more moderate daily life too.*

Q   **I had a brilliant 'retox' weekend but my wife was horrified as she's banned most of the foods I wanted to eat from the house. She wants me to promise not to do it again. What should I do?**

A   *Say no. That's a really unreasonable promise to want you to make. Unless you're endangering your health by constantly eating things that are bad for you, it is not acceptable to want you to live your life according to a map she's drawn up. Rebel! Stand up for your right to retox.*

Q   I'm a recovering alcoholic. This idea is simply dangerous. Do you agree?

A   Telling a recovering alcoholic to have a drink is dangerous and irresponsible and that's definitely NOT what I'm doing. Alcoholism and smoking are addictions and addictions are never healthy or fun. I know a member of Alcoholics Anonymous whose 'retox' weekend consists of a burger from a very greasy fast food joint near his home. For most of the month, he runs marathons and is in training and eating healthy, if calorific, meals but he really looks forward to missing training and eating junk on his weekend 'off'. He says it makes him really enjoy his normal routine afterwards.

50

12

Me, myself and I

Don't compare or compete with anyone but yourself. You're not a carbon copy of anyone – not even your identical twin, if you have one.

Each person on the planet is unique and we should celebrate that uniqueness by not constantly trying to measure up to somebody else.

The worst people for comparing themselves to others are overachievers. Instead of enjoying the successes and blessings they have had, they're too busy looking at the next target and this mindless dash to some imaginary finishing line that never comes. Will they be happy being the next Richard Branson? Hell, no! They don't want to be the 'next' anybody – they want to be the original, the one that people quote in business or reference books; the epitome of success.

The problem with being that sort of a person is that when life throws you a curve ball, you can be hit a lot harder than you'd expect. Redundancies happen, the business doesn't do as well as you thought it would, your loved one leaves and your supposedly 'perfect' marriage falls apart. Any manner of unexpected and unwelcome changes can happen. If you've spent your life living up to someone else's idea of success, it can be a terrible blow when that is taken away from you.

Here's an idea for you...

Channel your future self. This is an exercise you can do simply for fun. Relax your body and close your eyes for a minute, imagine that you're about 65 years old and about to retire (if you are that age then take it another 20 years forward). Then write down some questions about your life that you'd like answered by your future self. A typical question might be 'Did I live abroad at all?' and then try to see your future self answering that question for you. You don't have to put much store by it but it does open you up to the way you would like things to pan out.

I know someone who always brings up the subject of salaries whenever we meet. She seems to want to confirm, every time we meet, that she is earning more than any of our other friends. Now I know from where this stems; she had a very unhappy childhood whereby she was the poorest kid in school and she was often mocked for having a modest home and never having the latest things. Instead of rising above the psychological wounds of her childhood, she is attempting to repair them by achieving material success and then by comparing herself to her peer group to satisfy herself that she is not the 'poor kid' any more. For those in our circle who don't know her very well, her questions are starting to grate and they now avoid her because it feels like she's lording it over them. This is very sad as it is the exact opposite to her desired outcome – acceptance.

We all have benchmarks by which we measure success. It may be money, it may be how handsome and charming our lovers are or by how good we look. Since all of these things have no intrinsic value in themselves, we only learn of their value through comparison. I once had the unenviable task of choosing between two men. Both were gorgeous, both rich and both very clever. In the end I chose neither. Why? Because when I thought about them, I thought about the fact that they were rich and handsome rather than that I really loved them. I intuitively knew that those value judgements would go out the window when I met the right guy. I'd no longer be thinking whether my guy would impress my friends but whether I enjoyed his company and whether he made me laugh.

In the same way, you should measure your success not by whether it meets the criteria of others or society but by whether you're happy with it. Happiness for you could be a small doughnut shop in a busy part of town while for the guy down the road it may be a baked goods empire, providing doughnuts to supermarkets across the world.
You be the judge.

'Envy consists in seeing things never in themselves, but only in their relations. If you desire glory, you may envy Napoleon, but Napoleon envied Caesar, Caesar envied Alexander, and Alexander, I daresay, envied Hercules, who never existed.'
BERTRAND RUSSELL, philosopher and Nobel Laureate

Defining idea…

How did it go?

Q   My colleague just got promoted over me. I can't help feeling envious of her. How do I stop?

A   *First, accept what you're feeling and don't try to suppress it. Talk to a confidante and spill your heart out. Then congratulate your colleague and see if she'd be prepared to give you some pointers for your own success. If she did it, so can you.*

Q   My parents always compare me to my older sister and find me wanting. How do I get them to see that I'm not her?

A   *So many families have that problem and the first thing you must remember is that it's not done maliciously. Your parents want the best for you and if your sister has been a success, they probably see it more as holding up a role model for you rather than talking your choices down. You need to gently but firmly point out that your sister is not you and so does not have the same desires, needs and motivations as you.*

Q   I make silly amounts of money in the City but it's starting to leave me cold. How do I make a change?

A   *You're in a position that many would love to find themselves in – the world's your oyster and you can decide to do anything you want. I reckon you're probably more scared about what you'll say when your peers ask 'What are you doing nowadays?' and you don't have a big city corporation name on your lips. Don't be scared, living your dreams is better than any impressive-sounding job title.*

13

Less is more

Having a clearout is great for the soul and even better for your pocket so get sorting through all your possessions, remembering to only keep what's useful or beautiful.

It's not just Stepford wives that need a neat, tidy home — we all need to come back from the chaos of the world outside to a haven of beauty and order.

I have this fantasy. No, not the one where I'm a mermaid and Josh Holloway (the actor who plays Sawyer in *Lost* and who's in the Davidoff Cool Water ads) dives into the sea, accidentally startling me in the middle of a bath… 'Oh, Mr Holloway! But I am naked!'… ahem. Anyway, moving on, I have this fantasy that I will come home one day and everything will be pristine and orderly. It will be as if Jeeves came by on his leave from Bertie Wooster and cleaned and tidied the house from top to bottom. Clothes would be neatly pressed and put away. Paperwork would be in files convenient to locate. Surfaces would have very little on them and so be easy to dust and keep clean. Beautiful objets d'art and frames would adorn the house.

Here's an idea for you...

Pick an area of your house you have been avoiding decluttering, play one of your favourite albums and just begin. If it's not beautiful or useful, it gets the heave-ho. Most albums are under an hour long and you can stop as soon as the music stops. If at the end of the album, you want to keep going, pop on another album and keep going.

It's a fantasy because I'm a hoarder. I never think 'this is junk', I think 'I could use that for Christmas wrapping decoration' or 'this might be useful one day'. Of course that one day is never, ever likely to come. Unless of course you throw away said bit of junk, in which case, you'll find a need for it the very next day.

Sue Kay, author and professional declutterer, once had a session with me. She called a lot of my concerns 'negative thinking'. I assumed bad things would happen if I let go of my junk. I'd not be able to prove my existence without my hundreds of scraps of paper. Except why would anyone be trying to eradicate my existence? After all, I'm not a top spy. I kept two copies of everything I'd ever written, just in case one of the copies went missing, had coffee split on it or was burned to a cinder. My logical mind can grasp that if I have stuff piled up everywhere, it is much more likely to go missing or have coffee split on it. Plus I keep the two copies together and can't think of one occasion on which one would be burnt to a cinder while the other remained unscathed.

Sue did a two-hour session with me and cleared masses of things. We had a charity bag, a keep bag and a throw away bag. Sue seems to have a morbid terror of moths and, given the amount of silk I've lost to the little blighters over the years, I share her concerns. She explained that the more stuff I had, the less likely I could keep it all clean and the more likely things like moths would get at it.

By the end of the session, my room felt lighter, I had got rid of loads of unnecessary stuff and I had found some earrings to wear that I had forgotten I had. It was a lot like treasure hunting. Her cool, calm approach made everything go fast and I didn't linger over every little thing, paralysed by fear that I might throw away something useful. Reading is also a big problem for me when decluttering as I tend to get caught up reading some clipping I've kept or a magazine that must be read before it is donated to the doctor's surgery. Having Sue there meant I couldn't indulge this real 'time bandit' when it comes to decluttering. Find a 'tough love' friend who'll sit drinking coffee while you declutter. Ask him or her to stop you if it looks like you're about to start reading something instead of getting on with it.

'No person who can read is ever successful at cleaning out an attic.'
ANN LANDERS, American advice columnist

Defining idea…

How did
it go?

**Q   I've sorted out my paperwork but now I can't find anything and I
have to do my taxes – help!**

A   *OK, this often happens to me and you have to a bit of a detective as you're
trying to figure out what would have been the logical place for you to have
put something. Just remember that you, on some level, know exactly where
you've put things and sit and think where that might have been. Luckily I
think you're probably more rational than my friend who puts all her bills in
the bread bin, behind the cookies. Seriously, she does.*

**Q   I have a big box of my children's childhood clothes and toys. I
can't part with them as they have such lovely memories for me
and I'd like their children to have them. Is that too sentimental?**

A   *There's nothing wrong with sentimentality if you temper it with practical-
ity. I keep my youngest sister's bootie as it reminds me of how tiny her
little foot was, a lovely memory to retain now that she's a moody teenager
wearing big wedge heels. However, clothes and toys get dated and, by the
time your kids have their own, they'll probably want to buy new things.
Plus where are you going to keep this stuff? In an attic or shed? If so, dust
and cobwebs will probably get them. Your best bet is to pick one or two
small things like a cuddly toy and some socks and put them in a special
place where you can regularly clean and look after them. I think that's a
much better way of preserving your memories.*

14

Soul rage

How to deal with anger (without getting 25-to-life)?
Take a deep breath before you blow your top –
remember you're a person, not a firework.

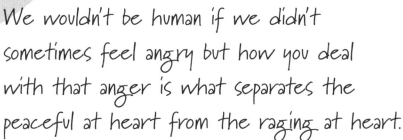

We wouldn't be human if we didn't sometimes feel angry but how you deal with that anger is what separates the peaceful at heart from the raging at heart.

My mate Simon trained as a Buddhist monk for several years in Thailand. This gives him a very calm and collected exterior and I have only ever heard him raise his voice once or twice in the whole time I've known him. His way of dealing with things is to laugh at the absurdity and then go get a mug of coffee. He rarely went into an all-out strop and rage about anything.

I used to vampire energy off him whenever I could. It was like sidling up to a fire and warming your hands. When you're naturally highly strung, meeting some-one who's not is a revelation. You have a blood vessel pounding in your forehead

Here's an idea for you... **Experiment with your food intake by keeping a food/emotion diary. Many people find their tempers calm down if they cut out red meat, and alkaline dairy products are also calming foods. If your diary shows you have a row whenever you have that medium-rare steak, it might be worth keeping it to special occasions when rows are less likely. Always, always drink a glass of water if you feel you're going to blow your top.**

because of something someone's said while your calm contemporary will simply say 'that's not really true, is it?' at the person talking nonsense. It is disarming.

Now please don't confuse Simon's composure with bottling things up. I am the expert on bottling things up. I used to go for years carrying rages in my stomach that I hadn't expressed. When I was 14 years old, I chased down a boy with a tennis racket with the intention of bludgeoning him to death with it because I had had enough of seven previous years of younger kids being cheeky at school. All that pent-up rage exploded and I'm pretty certain that if I hadn't been so bad at running, I would have swiftly ended my school career in a very newsworthy murder.

Anger in and of itself is not bad. If it was then you'd never have had the civil rights movement, women would never have got the vote, we would not have been able to remove corrupt leaders from our governments; quite a few good things have resulted from a well-placed sense of righteous anger. What's bad is when you hurt someone else – either emotionally or physically – because you're unable to express your anger appropriately.

We have tongues and lips to speak out our rage and to kiss and make up after having expressed it. When we feel angry with our partners, it is particularly difficult as they are the people we expect to spend the rest of our lives with. Just remember that an argument does not a break-up make. You can feel angry and you can row without it needing to reach critical levels. Your partner knows how to press your buttons better than anyone else so remember that before you fly off the handle.

Also, when you feel angry about something, consider first if there is anything constructive you can do about it. Write to your MP? Write a letter of complaint? Ask to see a manager? Go to marriage or career counselling? Once you've exhausted the constructive 'dealing with the problem' options, look at dealing with the emotion. Physical exercise tends to drain away anger like nothing else. So perhaps you could go for a swim or a walk? Above all, don't take your anger out on your friends and family. They are your support network and you should be kind to them. You know it makes sense.

Defining idea…

'Get mad, then get over it.'
COLIN POWELL, retired General and former US Secretary of State

How did it go?

Q **I can't let go of my anger at my aunt. She had no children of her own and she spent all her time criticising me and my brothers. How can I forgive her?**

A *It can be hard to forgive wounds inflicted on us when we're young but now that you're an adult, think about her motivations. If she didn't have children of her own, perhaps she was trying to be a parent to you and the only problem was that her parenting skills weren't that great. We rarely take the time to criticise those we have no interest in. See her attention to you as an indication of her love and concern and you'll be on the way to forgiveness.*

Q **I sometimes feel like throwing things around when I get into a rage and the other day my little girl flinched when I yelled at my husband. That really upset me. How do I control my temper?**

A   Apart from anger management courses, you can remove yourself from
     the situation and go for a short walk to calm down. Or consider taking up
     an energetic sport like boxing or martial arts to channel your aggression
     safely. If you start to feel out of control, speak to your GP who can also
     check for hormonal imbalance and advise on counselling services.

Q   **I never lose my temper but my husband says I'm passive-aggres-
     sive. What does he mean?**

A   Do you take on loads and then act the martyr for doing it all? Do you say
     things like 'Oh, I was hoping we could do this but if you don't want to, I
     understand'? On the face of it you seem very goody-two-shoes but on an
     energetic level it's as bad as if you were seething and having a go. I'm not
     saying that is the case as I don't know you but maybe it's something to
     think about?

15

Animal love

No, not seductive sheep in suspenders, finding unconditional love in perfect pets. And, of course, the not-so-perfect ones.

A love of animals is something to be encouraged in children and adults alike as it teaches you compassion, caring and the ancient art of cuddling.

We all know that stroking a cat can lower your blood pressure and studies have found that even autistic children who don't like to be touched will respond to animals positively. There is something incredibly lovable about a creature that won't judge or criticise you but will just be there for you.

One of my pet (fnarr-fnarr!) hates is when people anthropomorphise animals and act as if they were like children. Pets aren't children; step away from the tu-tu and tiara for your pug dog. We should appreciate the doggy qualities of a dog: loyal, lives in the present moment, usually quite greedy and loves sniffing everything. The catty qualities of a cat: disdain, agility, curiosity and good grooming habits. We should appreciate these animals and others for what they are rather than wanting

Here's an idea for you...

Have a conversation with your pet. Not just 'who's a lovely-jubbly lickle puddy cat?'-style conversations but proper ones where you tell them what's happening in your life and tell them about future walks or plans that include them. Of course they won't reply and occasionally they'll look at you as if you're stark raving mad but there is something very cathartic about explaining why he won't agree to marry you to your goldfish. They make a very wise bubbly sound in response to your blubbing.

them to react in a way that is uniquely human (I mean it, I don't care how schweet it is, put the pink tu-tu down).

One of the doggiest dogs I've ever known was owned by one of my exes. It was called Bart and it was a young St. Bernard who was convinced he was a lap dog. I'm no Paris Hilton but that didn't stop Bart from attempting to get into my handbag whenever I visited. Walking with Bart was terrific exercise as it was the only way to get truly horizontal in the air without the aid of NASA as he pulled you along at high speed. He loved other dogs. He loved lamp posts. He especially loved pavements. And cars. And traffic wardens. And discarded bits of paper. And of course, excrement. He adored excrement. There was nothing that didn't make this dog thrilled to be alive. I learnt more from a summer of looking after him than I did from a lifetime of workshops with spiritual gurus.

Pets can teach us a lot and they can also mellow us out. My nan used to breed tropical fish. My earliest memories of her were of someone quite scary and forbidding. My mother confirms that her mum wasn't exactly tactile with her grandchildren but her soft spot was fish. Ma says that if they had ever upset her and she wasn't talking to one of the kids, they'd head to the aquarium before coming home, and would give her a present of a new fish as a peace offering. When she was tending her fish, she was relaxed and happy.

My youngest sister has inherited a love of fish from my nan. Hers are goldfish and you'd think a goldfish doesn't really do much but she's invented games that she plays with them, she talks to them and is very conscientious about cleaning out their tank and feeding them on time. This is why I think fish are the best animal for a young child to have as a pet; you learn how to care for something outside yourself and the danger of your pet biting the next door neighbour is somewhat minimised.

Living in the city keeping pets can be a bit difficult, especially if you live in an apartment. The way that I've got round that is with a love of horses and horse riding. You can do this anywhere there are stables; we used to live near an inner city stable and you could ride the horses in local areas of greenery. Best of all is riding when on holiday as you meet a new animal, get some exercise and explore new sights.

If none of these animal delights appeal to you, consider appreciating the beauty of cows and sheep in the countryside on a weekend break. Springtime when the lambs are jumping around in the fields is particularly lovely. Just don't blame me if you decide to become a vegetarian afterwards.

'All of the animals except for man know that the principle business of life is to enjoy it.'
SAMUEL BUTLER, writer and poet

Defining idea…

67

How did it go?

Q **My cat hates my boyfriend and hisses and spits whenever he's about of an evening. I love my cat and my boyfriend. How do I reconcile them?**

A *Start by making a fuss of your cat when your boyfriend's around so your cat knows that you won't abandon her but also start to subtly introduce your boyfriend into your cat's life. Ask your boyfriend to get your cat's evening meal and have him put it down in front of her so that she knows that he will be someone who's sticking around. I hope he's nice though, as sometimes animals have an uncanny knack of spotting the lying, cheating toad.*

Q **My wife is allergic to cat and dog hair so we can't have any pets like that but I really miss having an animal to pet. Any suggestions?**

A *A tortoise? Perhaps a snake, if you're not afraid of them. Iguanas are very lovely as are lizards but some of them might attack your wife when she's menstruating as the smell is similar to female iguanas and lizards on heat. If your wife is reading this, she may be feeling a little faint by now. The best compromise is probably fish as, even though you can't pet them, they're capable of a surprising degree of companionship.*

16

Say it till you mean it

Affirmations to live by (and non-embarrassing ways to use them). Repeating words of comfort and hope can actually bring you comfort and hope.

The universe wants to deliver lots of lovely goodies to you but you have to give it your shopping list and you may have to repeat it a few times just to drive the point home.

I believe in mermaids, fairies and little green men from Mars. However, in all the time I've explored mind, body and spirit ideas, I've never believed in affirmations. I mean, how on earth can repeating patently untrue statements to yourself ever work? It sounded like so much New Age bunkum that I didn't give it another thought.

Then one day, I met a lady called Helen Wingstedt. I trusted Helen because through her psychic horse companions (stay with me here, we'll be out of the twilight zone shortly), she had pinpointed a lot of my problems within an hour of meeting me. Helen is a fan of affirmations and she gave me rather a good one: 'I choose to be

Here's an idea for you...

Write out a favourite affirmation on a small slip of paper and slip it into your bra (gentleman, try a pocket rather than anything unhygienic). Then each time you have a loo break during your working day, slip out the affirmation and whisper it to yourself. You can say it completely silently if you're scared someone from accounting might overhear and get the wrong idea.

loving and trusting'. This is because at the time I met her I was not at all loving and trusting. I was cynical and tired of people messing me about. Anyway, like I said, I trusted her and so I started to repeat this to myself silently all the time.

A very strange thing started to happen. People started to smile at me. Complete strangers, men, women and children – smiling for no apparent reason. My first instinct was to check whether my flies were undone (they weren't) and my second was to get suspicious about an invasion of body-snatching, smiling aliens (still inconclusive). The point is that the universe was responding to the affirmation I was putting out there. The universe thought I was loving and trusting, not because I was but because I was affirming that as my intent. In the same way, affirming 'I have plenty of time to do everything I need to get done' will miraculously create vast swathes of time in your day in which you can get your stuff done. 'I am healthy and energetic' will yield those results, even if you're sick when you're affirming it.

Try to avoid negatives in your affirmations so nothing like 'I am free from pain,' as the universe is literalist and will see the word 'pain' without seeing the context

of 'free from'. It would be better to say 'I
am happy and healthy,' as presumably you
wouldn't be very happy or healthy if you were
in pain. The other thing to remember is to
keep your affirmation present. It's no good
saying 'I will be happy in my job,' you need
'I am happy in my job'. This is because, like I said, the universe is literalist and will
appreciate that your grammar means that you're not feeling happy right now but
will in the future. Since the future is never now, you can't achieve what you need
right now.

'Happiness is the longing for repetition.'
MILAN KUNDERA, author

Defining idea...

Also remember not to be so specific that you end up messing up your own wish.
If you say 'I am loved by Paul Smith of 14 Heyford Close', you open up a whole can
of worms. Mr Smith's dad, also Paul, may visit within the week and take a shine to
you. Better to say 'I am romantically loved and cherished and I return that love,' or
something a bit less wordy but you get my drift?

Once you've worded a nice, juicy affirmation, start saying it all the time under
your breath. No-one needs to hear this or needs to know what you're up to. Just be
discreet and keep doing it. If discretion isn't something you're bothered about, try
writing your affirmation out and sticking it on desk where you can see it. Or typing
it out as a screensaver or having it stuck next to your shaving mirror. Basically try
and see those words as often as possible and say them to yourself as often as possible too. You'll be amazed at the results.

How did it go?

Q   I did an affirmation 'I will be rich very soon' for a week and it hasn't worked. Why?

A   *Because you phrased it in the future so you're constantly waiting for 'very soon' to arrive. Try 'I am very rich' and then remember that 'rich' can refer to having loving family and friends, a good social life and excellent health as well as millions in the bank.*

Q   I always feel silly and 'New Agey' doing these. It's just not my style. Any other suggestions?

A   *When you were learning to read, did you feel silly for not knowing what letter had which sound? And did you think reading was just a bourgeois affectation? Of course not! So, if you want to harness the power of affirmations, you have to get over any embarrassment and just do them in your head. Why is your internal social critic so strong? Silence him or her by doing them anyway. If you really can't face it, well, no-one is forcing you, so onwards and upwards.*

Q   It worked! It worked really well and I told my best friend about it but she thinks I've turned into some Madonna-wannabe now and refuses to discuss it with me. What should I do?

A   *Nothing. You can lead a horse to water but you can't make it affirm 'I drink water to my heart's content'. Let her have her beliefs and you have yours.*

17

List lustre

Lists can bring order into your life and mind – but only if you use them wisely, young Padwan.

The beauty of writing a list is that you can tick it off and have a visual reminder of how much you have achieved in the day.

My friend Alex could probably sort out world peace if she was given a pad, a pen, a bit of time and a free hand. She is the list genius. I once made the mistake of telling her how overwhelmed by work I felt.

'Right,' she announced, in the manner of one about to go to war. 'Get me my pad and start telling me what you have to do.' She sat there and made a list of everything I had to do over the course of that month. She then went through and prioritised it. I tend to do a lot of favours for my ex – probably in the hope that he'll fall back in love with me. His bits and pieces were the first to be chopped from Alex's master list. 'Only do that which you have a good reason to do. If you're struggling to find time to do the tasks that earn you your money, you do not have time to do tasks that are just about emotional unfinished business'. Of course, she was right and her red pen is a great deal more lethal than any sword and several boys had been beheaded metaphorically by the end of the list-making.

Here's an idea for you...

Right before you go to bed, make a wish list. During the day we are so busy with work lists that we forget that you can use the power of the list to manifest lovely, fun things too. Choose something enjoyable like beach holidays or books or restaurants you'd like to visit and make a list of the top ten you'd really like to have or do. Then when each happens, cross it off your list. When the last is done, make a new list!

While we were working on this 'master list', Alex told me about one of her friends who was very like me. She had a beautiful mahogany dining table that she never got to eat at or even see properly because it was groaning under the weight of all her paperwork, magazines and projects. Alex sorted it out for her by refusing to let her handle one piece of paper more than once. Like me, her friend was used to picking things up, going 'oh I must do that' and then putting it down again and going onto the next thing. By the end she was left with everything still undone but Alex changed all that.

If a piece of paper had a phone number or address on it that she needed, it was to be copied down into her contacts book straight away and the paper could go in the recycling bin. Old newspapers went straight to the recycling bank because it was old news and not worth reading. If a paper reminded her friend of something she had to do, it was written down on the master list. Anything to be filed had to be filed then and there, with a new filing system created to deal with the bits of paper. By the end, she had a clear, beautifully polished table and one list containing all the information about what she had to do.

Alex then told her friend (and me) to go through each thing, in priority order, and just do it. Once done, tick it off. At the end of the day, we had to transfer any unfinished tasks onto the next day's list. It was a very satisfying thing and, since I've started doing this, I get through so much more and have such a great sense of achievement and – yes, you've guessed it – inner peace.

'**Nothing is so fatiguing as the eternal hanging on of an uncompleted task.'**
WILLIAM JAMES, American
psychologist and philosopher

Defining
idea...

How did it go?

Q **The second my list is almost done, someone comes along and adds another 10 things to it! How do I catch up?**

A *I once said almost the exact same thing to my mate, Heathcliffe. Heathcliffe, who apart from having the coolest name in the world is also very wise, laughed and said 'If you finished everything there was to do, what would be the point of living any more? You'd be done, finished, sorted.' And he's right. That to do list isn't a bunch of chores, it's the business of living and, if you're alive, there will always be more to do. Don't let it overwhelm you, just take one thing at a time.*

Q **Each day I transfer what's left undone to my next day's list but the same things linger on the list. How do I find the time to do the undone?**

A *There is an organisational guru called Brian Tracy and Brian has a phrase called 'swallow the frog'. This means that you should do the thing you're most reluctant to do first so that you'll have 'swallowed the frog' in the morning and can continue to more pleasant tasks for the rest of the day. It seems like the thing that remains undone is your frog as you keep putting it off so go swallow it now.*

Q **I'm about to go on holiday and my to-do list is never-ending. Should I cancel my break?**

A *That's a trick question, right? You can't seriously be considering cancelling your holiday in order to do more things. If you're serious, you need to sit down and give yourself a stern talking-to. You have a finite amount of time between now and when you go on holiday. Do your best but don't be unrealistic. If you can't do it all, you simply can't.*

18

The art of doing nothing

Some days it's best to just stay under your duvet. Try to convince your family to move in with you and make a teepee of fun for the day.

Retreating from the world is a restorative and something you should definitely do as regularly as you can.

We're funny creatures, aren't we? We get two weeks' holiday maybe twice a year and we try and fill it with as much as humanly possible. Yet the most relaxing holiday I've ever had was right here at home when I was waiting on a contract for something and so couldn't leave the country. I spent most of the week reading in bed, like I used to do as a child. I even had my little sister bring me up toast and tea and the occasional chocolate bar so I wouldn't have to leave my little huddle of joy.

Someone once said 'We are human beings, not human doings' and, you know, who-ever it was is quite right. Sometimes you just need to be rather than do. Being can involve contemplation or it can involve nothing more exerting than just vegging out and grunting in response to others for a day or so.

Here's an idea for you...

If you're a particularly social person, try a month of accepting no invitations. No parties, cinema trips, dinners or sports dates. And don't invite anyone to yours either. A whole month of abstinence will make you realise how much leisure time you actually have and you can then use it wisely after your month's fast to choose just those activities that truly make you happy rather than those you do out of a sense of obligation.

You can't continuously behave in this way as then you'd be a person apart from society and, well, you'd probably be wanting to find yourself a mountain somewhere rather than read books on inner peace. However, you can occasionally opt out of it all. You can say 'I'm not going to work. I'm not getting dressed. I'm not doing anything.' In the States, they have a very honest concept called 'duvet days'; here in the UK, we have the time-honoured tradition of the 'sickie'. I'm not advocating lying to the people who pay your wages, merely negotiate a duvet day with your boss (perhaps a day off in lieu of weekend or overtime work?).

Also think about all the non-work things you do: the shopping, the housework, the helping with homework, the personal grooming, the buying of presents, the social engagements, the dinner parties and the weekend breaks. Are you exhausted yet? I'm feeling like I need a lie-down just looking at that list. We seem to be hell-bent on filling every single moment of time with something useful. If we're not doing all that then we're on the computer, emailing friends that we haven't seen in ages. And why haven't we seen them? Because we're too busy!

'Sitting quietly, doing nothing, spring comes, and the grass grows by itself.'

Zen proverb

Defining idea...

Then when we do get around to seeing our friends, we feel compelled to have interesting things to tell them about so we run to the latest exhibition or to see a movie and a lot of it is geared toward remaining 'current' rather than true enjoyment. And so it goes on and on.

I remember a saner time. A time when, as a child, there was nothing to do so we just hung out. We'd walk down to the park or we'd go and collect conkers in the churchyard or we'd just sit on a wall and wait for the ice cream van. I'm the last person to hark back to a nostalgic, bygone era but I do think we've lost the art of doing nothing much in particular.

My friend the occult artist and hellraiser, Joel Biroco, describes a lot of what he does as 'the art of doing nothing'. This is because he actually lives Zen philosophy while others just study it. He often just sits there, not doing much in particular apart from just being. The end result of these years of just being? A pretty amazing human being with a great deal of interesting knowledge and experience.

How did it go?

Q   I felt so guilty doing nothing that I went on a cleaning spree in the kitchen. Is that bad?

A   *Cleaning can be fun and pottering around the house is a 'doing' way of 'doing nothing'. The most important thing is not to feel guilty. Don't feel guilty about sitting doing nothing and don't feel guilty about getting up and cleaning the kitchen. Just chill.*

Q   My son has no job and no prospects and sits around the house all day doing nothing. Surely that isn't going to find him inner peace?

A   *Well, it won't because clearly we have to pay for stuff in life like food, clothes, rent and if he's not doing anything, at some point he will feel the pinch of not having money for that which he wants. Don't bill-roll his lifestyle and try to have open discussions about what he would like to do in life. Don't impose your ideas of what would be useful or good for him, let him decide. He may surprise you yet.*

Q   I never feel like doing anything. I just want to stay asleep under my duvet forever but it doesn't really make me happy. What's going on?

A   *I'm no doctor so I can't say for sure but that sounds more like depression than the art of doing nothing. The lack of drive that accompanies a bout of depression is one of the most crippling things about it. Please do go and see your GP if this continues as nobody deserves to spend their lives wanting to be in a cocoon rather than out there in the world.*

19

Live forever

An old Chinese proverb says that you gain a day in longevity for every new thing you try. Why not see how many extra days you can clock up?

New-fangled stuff shouldn't unnerve you as trying new things is the way we stay young at heart and interested in life.

While at university, my friends kept asking me if I had an email address. 'Don't be silly,' I said. 'It'll never catch on. I much prefer a letter.' Thankfully I'm not a future trend predictor as emails definitely did catch on. I do still prefer a letter but I can also laugh at my foolish younger self who had no idea how much time I'd spend in the future on email and the internet.

The latest new thing I've been (unsuccessfully) resisting is social networking websites. They eat up time and they're intrusive and annoying. Of course I did still have to log on and try them, though, as I am pathologically attracted to new experiences.

Here's an idea for you...

Today find a recipe that you've never tried before (it can be a very simple assembling one if you're a hopeless cook) and make it tonight. Better still, invent something of your own. A distinct and fabulous cuisine called 'Indo-Chinese' developed when Indian and Chinese chefs in North India took the techniques and ingredients of Chinese cooking and combined them with Indian spicing so don't be afraid of adding your own touch.

Nowhere is this more prevalent than with food. I have eaten crocodile, snake, frog's legs, alligator, several varieties of deer and all manner of insects and crustaceans. Basically, if anything has moved near me, I've tried to eat it. This adventurousness in food also extends to other areas and so most weeks I'm writing articles on everything from vampire hunters to 1940s knitwear.

My friends and I try to discover new favourite restaurants and bars when we go out so that we're not constantly going to the same places. There's no harm in having your favourite 'local' but if you start to find your bum fits rather too snugly into your favourite seat or stool, it's time to find another haunt, my friend.

Occasionally you will find that you try something new, a new dish, say, and it's so awful, you want to gag. This is also good because you can chalk that down to experience and know never to order it again. Think of a baby. His instinct is to shove everything he gets his hands on into his mouth and if his hands contain nothing, then they're going in there instead. Everything is explored through touch and taste. We become jaded because we start to make assumptions about what is good and what is bad. Trying the new puts us back in 'baby' mode and it can be a very exciting time.

'Do not go where the path may lead; go instead where there is no path and leave a trail.'

RALPH WALDO EMERSON

Defining idea…

The benefit of all this interest in the new and untried is that a) you never get bored and b) you can sing for your supper. People tend to do pretty much the same things as their peers and the ones they gravitate towards are those who push the boundaries of what is the usual.

My friend is an 80-year-old shamanic healer and she's spent years studying plant medicine in the Amazon. She can't stand talking to most people her own age as they are very constricted in the things they will talk about. 'I don't want to know about health problems and grandchildren,' she says, bluntly. 'I want to know about the nature of the world, how people can heal and be healed. I want to know what the stars are made of, rather than what the stock market is doing to their investments'. I do believe that Iona will one day find out what the stars are made of as she is completely unstoppable in finding out what everything else is made of!

How did it go?

Q **I suggested a few new things for me and my wife to try in the bedroom but she was 'disgusted and appalled' and now I feel embarrassed for having asked. What should I do?**

A *Oh dear! Our sexual preferences are probably one of the most individual things about us so what rocks one person's boat may not do so for another. However, a healthy relationship is one in which you can discuss your likes, dislikes and curiosities without feeling judged by your lover. Explain to your wife how you feel and make it clear that this discussion is not a pre-cursor to nagging her about trying new things but is merely an attempt at more openness in the relationship.*

Q **My husband won't leave the house or try anything new, not even a new pasta sauce. I'm at my wits' end, I'm so bored. What should I do?**

A *What's stopping you trying new things without him? Cook that new pasta sauce and settle down to enjoy every bite while he looks on eating his same-old, same-old. I bet the smell and look entices him enough to try at least one bite. Start small like this and when he sees you traipsing off to your salsa class every week, he's bound to want to get in on some of the fun.*

Q **New things make me nervous as I had some tremendous upheavals in my youth and I don't want to feel anchorless again. Am I too stuck in my ways?**

A *You have fear and that's only normal when you're talking about stepping out of your comfort zone. Take it easy on yourself and try one tiny new thing each week. It may be a new brand of bread or perhaps a tie in a different colour to the one you normally wear. Little and often will do to spice up your life as much as the big changes.*

20

When all else fails, have a bath

Bathing can be the best and most sensual way to achieve inner harmony. Just avoid razors.

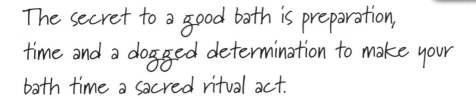

The secret to a good bath is preparation, time and a dogged determination to make your bath time a sacred ritual act.

It takes me ages to get ready for my bath. First I have to find my special expensive bath oils. These are kept in the bedroom as steam and water makes the capsules melt so they can only be taken down to pop in the bath and the box then has to be taken back to my dresser. I then have to find the fluffiest towel in the house. I bought one from a big, posh hotel chain once (no, I didn't steal it from the room, I'm a very good girl, I'll have you know!). Then there are the scented candles. I also have some bath lights that light up on contact with water.

Here's an idea for you...

Can you safely put a radio or CD player in your bathroom? Keeping it away from the water (actually, you can get shower radios now), play some music while you're having your bath. My favourite bathing music is 80s pop, mostly Wham! and Duran Duran because you don't have to pretend to be cool when you're naked with yourself.

Finally I have to select a good book or magazine. It must not be taxing and I must not get upset if it gets wet. I usually like to read Sarah Ban Breathnach's books in the bath. The woman is a complete sensualist and writes about beauty and aesthetics with a great deal of grace. I always want to make things with cinnamon in when I read her stuff.

By the time I get into my hot bath, the mood is set for an hour's soak in sensual pleasure. I tend to stay in the bath until my fingers get wrinkly. I wish we were more waterproof as then I could stay even longer.

I think up my best ideas in the bath. I don't allow anyone to hurry me out of my bath because my bath is sacrosanct. It is a ritual of caretaking for the soul that I won't ever forget to do. When I was a teenager, my parents attempted to shame me out of my daily bath. 'Do you have any idea how much water you're wasting?' 'Yep,' I replied nonchalantly. Then, because I did feel a little ashamed, I started washing my handwash stuff in the bath water, after I'd finished with my bath. It was still a tremendous waste in comparison to a shower but I don't drive and I don't own a car so I think that this luxury should be mine for the taking.

Baths are also used in many spiritual traditions as ways to cleanse negative influence and attractive fresh, wonderful things for the bather. Santero Elliot Rivera is a priest of Santeria, a West African religious tradition that is practised throughout the world, and I met him for a divination reading once. Santero Elliot struck me as one of the nicest people I have ever met. A Santeria shell divination is done by casting cowrie shells and then interpreting what will happen by how they fall. In my reading, Santero Elliot described my work situation to me exactly. He then gave me the recipe for a white cleansing bath. I was to take the white of an egg, some florida water (a cologne you can find in any Afro-Caribbean shop), the petals of some white flowers (not roses) and some water and mix it all together and leave it with a white cloth over it overnight. Then in the morning, I was to bathe with that water and then have my usual bath/shower.

By the morning, the water was freezing and I yelped pouring it over my head. But it did smell divine. Then I had my usual bath envisaging white, sparkly energy coming in through my crown and pouring out through every pore. After that I had my shower and went to work. I had the most amazing day. A number of difficulties disappeared with ease. Now, whenever, I feel stressed or under attack, I take that healing bath taught to me by Santero Elliot and suddenly the world seems a whole lot better.

'There must be quite a few things that a hot bath won't cure, but I don't know many of them.'

SYLVIA PLATH, author

Defining idea...

93

How did it go?

Q   **I definitely prefer showers. Can I find inner peace in a shower?**

A   *You certainly can! Showers of water have negative ions, those little particulars that make us feel happier and healthier. One of the most peaceful experiences I have ever had involved being behind a waterfall in Somerset. The spray on my face felt wonderful. Enjoy your showers and don't let us bath fascists tell you what to do.*

Q   **I'm now of an age that I find it difficult to get into a bath and I really miss them. Any ideas?**

A   *There are now some fantastic mobility baths about in which you sit on a chair and the bath fills up around you, a bit like a hot tub. In some cases, your local council can subsidise putting such mobility devices in. Have a shop around, there are definitely things out there to support your love of bathing.*

Q   **I'm afraid I'll fall asleep in the bath and drown. Is this a rational fear?**

A   *After watching Nightmare on Elm Street, it is a perfectly rational fear but the truth is that you're likely to wake up if you end up under water as your body is geared toward keeping you alive and it would notice if your breathing was suddenly impaired. If a dunking frightens you though, how about an inflatable neck cushion? Very handy things.*

21

Clean and serene

Don't despair, reach for the duster of dharma and clean your way to a calm, steady disposition.

Cleaning isn't boring, kids, cleaning can be your friend — oh yes it can!

I'm not sure when my cleaning fetish began. It may have been when I first saw my beloved's kitchen. His whole house was achingly beautiful and caked in dirt. It was exactly the way I'd want my own house to be, except dirty. So I set about cleaning it. I cleaned till I turned my hands red raw. I cleaned till I could see my face in the reflection on surfaces. I cleaned till I had found (and kept) £7.50 down the back of his sofa.

He turned up, looked around, said this looks nice, and proceeded to mess it all up again. That was when I realised that cleaning is not a destination, it is a journey. Many a woman (and man) have lost themselves in the idea that you have to keep things pristine all the time in order for them to be clean. If you do that, you'll be exhausted all the time.

Here's an idea for you... **Spend the next very sunny day cleaning the car by hand or alternatively your ground floor windows. Enlist the help of your partner or kids and make it go faster with a cold beer (or homemade lemonade) or two. If you ensure any chores are done in the spirit of fun, both you and your family will want to do them again. Also, spend the money you would have spent on a car wash or window cleaner on a DVD and some popcorn as a reward for all your hard work.**

No, you have to turn to Hindu religious texts to sort this one out. On the eve of an impossible battle, Lord Krishna spoke to Arjuna the warrior king and explained the concept of dharma or caste duty. Dharma means that if you're a warrior, the winning or losing isn't your problem, it's the fighting that matters. You are duty-bound to fight.

In modern terms this means that the end result of your actions is not what is important, it's conscientiously carrying them out. I know, I know, it's a bit of a stretch to ask you to imagine that Lord Krishna was referring to bed-making when he talked of dharma but there is a case for saying, don't fret too much that they'll have to be re-made tomorrow and the day after tomorrow and the day after that ad nauseam. Just get on with it in a spirit of being in the moment.

I find cleaning really therapeutic. I can lose myself in the grain of wood as I'm polishing it. I can see rainbow worlds in bubbles when I'm doing the washing up. Admittedly I can't see much in a dirty oven but hey, it's great exercise to be scrubbing away on your knees. OK, I can see I haven't sold you on that last one.

The other important thing to remember is that your family and you are in it together so don't feel like you have to do everything. No-one will do you for child labour if you get the kids to occasionally undertake a little light dusting and even toddlers can be taught to put their toys away in a toy box when they're done playing. My sister, who is a phenomenally good mother, taught her kids from a very early age to be responsible for their own toys. Because we were spoilt by how pliable her little ones were, other people's children and their capacity to wreak havoc left us reeling in horror.

'We are not afraid to look under the bed, or to wash the sheets; we know that life is messy. We know that somebody has to clean it up, and that only if it is cleaned up can we hope to start over, and get better.'
MARSHA NORMAN, novelist and Pulitzer Prize-winning playwright

Defining idea...

Still, even if you can't get your little ones in on the act, your life partner can definitely do his bit. Split your chores according to personal preferences or attribute each chore a number 1–6 and throw a dice to decide who does what. Introduce an element of fun into your cleaning and you'll soon be relaxing with a glass of wine, surveying your clean and serene domain.

How did it go?

Q   **I recycle and care about green issues but a lot of cleaning products are terrible for the environment and our bodies. What can I do?**

A   *There are now several 'eco' ranges out there that do a great cleaning job, without all the harsh chemicals. And, if you have a bit of time, you can also research ways of using natural household things such as vinegar, lemon juice and the like in your cleaning.*

Q   **I think there are better things to do with my time than cleaning. Surely volunteering or working is a better use of my time?**

A   *Volunteering is great, as is work, but without nurturing your home for at least part of the week, you send out the message that you're not as important as other people. It may seem boring or repetitive – heck, it often is – but when you take care of your home and your things, you let the universe know that you are worth looking after too. So don't short-change yourself with slovenliness.*

Q   **I hate it, I hate it, I hate it! I don't want to clean, please help?**

A   *Can you afford to hire someone to do it for you? If you can, then do that. Alternatively, look at bartering your services. Perhaps you're brilliant at making cakes or DIY? Swap with family and friends so that they do your cleaning and you do the things they don't want to do. If you really can't bear cleaning, try also to keep your possessions to a minimum as then you won't have as much to clean.*

22

Guilt be gone

Kick guilt to the kerb. Unless you're a serial killer.

Guilt can be one of the most useless emotions out there and the sooner you can excise it from your life, the better.

Guilt exists for one purpose only, to flag up when we've done something wrong that we should feel bad about. It is our moral centre kicking us in the backside for perceived wrong-doing. It is our conscience pricking us to make amends. It exists to ensure we're nicer people who don't treat others in a way that would be considered cruel or hurtful. However, there is another type of guilt that has nothing to do with morality or right and wrong. It's a false guilt that is the result of your inability to forgive yourself for not doing what's expected of you. Do not succumb to that second sort of guilt.

Do you often do things out of a need to avoid feeling guilty? Make phone calls, maintain friendships with people you don't really like, sign up to make charity donations you can't really afford, agree to do things for the Parent Teacher Association because you don't want to seen as not pulling your weight? Such a widespread

Here's an idea for you... **Excise the word 'sorry' from your phone conversations for a week. You won't be able to do it because it is actually impossible. Try it and you'll see. Imagine what a conversation without 'sorry' sounds like: 'I couldn't come to your wedding. I hope you had a good time.' Saying that will sound to your ears as if you're calling the mother of the bride a crack ho. The conditioning is very, very strong and you'll be hard pressed not to say the 's' word but try anyway and may the force be with you.**

misuse of guilt has to be halted. We need to appreciate the true reasons for guilt and, as long as you're not a felon, you really don't need to feel half as much guilt as you probably do.

The best way out of having guilt as your motivating factor in doing things is to learn the liberating effect of just saying 'no'. Most children go through a phase, at around the age of two, where they will start yelling 'NO!' in response to just about everything. That's why they call it 'the terrible twos' but psychologists reckon we all go through this phase as this is the first time we start to see ourselves as separate individuals and so we experiment with asserting an independent will. If you are to effectively get rid of guilt, you'll have to revert to this stage for a bit. You also need to experiment to find out what is your true will and what has simply been imposed upon you through an attempt to avoid guilt.

The next time someone asks you to do something, say 'let me check and get back to you'. That way you're buying time to consider whether you do actually want to do it. We often respond to things hurriedly, in a fluster, and then have to cancel afterwards – causing us more guilt for having let someone down. Even if you don't cancel it, having to do something because you couldn't think of a reason/excuse on the spot to say 'no' will only leave you feeling resentful and 'put upon' later. So buy yourself that time to respond.

'Guilt: the gift that keeps on giving.'
ERMA BOMBECK, American humorist and columnist

Defining idea...

Before you start to feel too guilty about anything, ask yourself whether you could have helped what happened. If you could have, well, it's too late now, it's in the past. All you can do is offer a heartfelt apology and find a way to make amends. Wringing your hands about it won't transport you back to that time when you could have done things differently. So it's now time to move forward.

We are often a lot more compassionate toward the guilty feelings of others than those of our own. If a friend feels guilty for letting down a member of her family, we comfort her and tell her to stop beating herself up about it. No such nice words of solace for our own selves. The next time you feel unduly bad about something, think about what you'd say if a friend was in that position. Would you hate her for not being able to do x, y or z? Of course not! So give yourself the same break.

How did it go?

Q **My sister always makes me feel guilty for not looking after her kids as much as her friend's sister does for her friend. She says I'm a bad aunt. Am I?**

A *You know to what degree you want involvement in your nieces' lives and if you don't want much, well, you're not their parent so you have the luxury of choice. Don't be bullied into doing something that you'll only resent doing and, as a result, probably do badly.*

Q **I had a fight with my best friend and I said some pretty horrible things. I tried to apologise but she doesn't want to know and I feel so guilty. What should I do?**

A *Leave her to calm down for a while. You've apologised and that's all you can do for now. Keep sending her the occasional card or making the occasional phone call. If your friendship is strong, she will eventually soften.*

Q **I did some pretty awful things as a teenager – joyriding, graffiti and the like – but I'm now working as a manager in a car sales showroom and I'm starting to make something of myself but my family won't let me forget my past. How do I get them to see I've changed?**

A *Actions speak louder than words and it looks like you're doing all you can to convince them. If they're still clinging to some previous notion of you, that's their problem. People change and jumping out of the pigeon-hole you've been put in is a tough thing to do – well done for trying!*

23

Booking in peace

A good book can be a companion that lets you leave the workaday world behind.

Losing yourself in a book is one of the few times you can travel anywhere and not worry about baggage or passports.

Think about the history of the humble book. People have been killed for writing books. Some books themselves have been burned and banned. Despite this being the age of the ghost-written, 12-year-old footballer's autobiography, we still attach a degree of respect to books. We expect books to have substance and be somewhat timeless, in a way that magazines and newspapers aren't.

Worryingly, in the UK today, in some areas one in five children leaving primary school can't read. This is one of the greatest tragedies in our country as reading sets you free. If you're having a bad or boring time of it, picking up a good book is like Alice going down the rabbit hole – you're bound to have an adventure.

However, the sheer number of books that are released each year can make choosing what to read more stressful than it need be. Should you listen to Richard & Judy or will your snobbish friends laugh at you for allowing TV presenters to choose your reading material? Should you ask at the local library what might be good to read?

Here's an idea for you...

Get a day pass for a seriously good library that covers the subjects you're especially interested in. Treat it like an outing and read not for work or study but for pleasure, surfing the books like you do the internet. I am interested in occult subjects and the Harry Price Library of Magical Literature is my library of choice. Find the library considered best for your own interests and immerse yourself in knowledge.

Books can change your life but they require the commitment of time, in both the hunting out of good ones and in the reading of them. So choosing the right book is a bit like choosing the right relationship, you have to like it enough to commit to it. I used to be a bit crab-like in both books and relationships; I'd cling on to the bitter, bitter end instead of abandoning and walking away if things were clearly not going to work out. I couldn't dump a book mid-way through, even if that meant dedicating a day to a book that I was clearly not enjoying. The day this all came to an end was when I spent a whole weekend reading a truly dreadful stream-of-consciousness number about an Indian woman and her Iranian husband. The book rambled on and on like a bad dream until eventually we got some action on – and I kid you not – the last paragraph where after reams and reams of philosophical musings about love, sex, race etc., etc. the husband kills her lover. I cheered and wished that the husband had killed the protagonist too. And the author. And me, for having read it right till the end.

Apart from culling bad books from your life, actively seek out the good ones. Ask your friends for recommendations and note who was most successful in suggesting a book you liked and stick to asking them. Consider joining a book club. This is the age of the funky book club so pick one near you and it will be a chance to meet new people as well as read more widely. Keep a reading diary and note what books you read and when, it becomes like a journal of where you've been in your imagination.

'I have always imagined that Paradise will be a kind of library.'

JORGE LUIS BORGES

Defining idea...

It's a bit sad that everyone on the tube is usually reading the latest big blockbuster and there's very little variety. It feels like being spoon-fed things from the publishing, retail and marketing industries. There is something to be said for safe choices though. I adore self-help books but I'd never read them in public as they have garish covers and titles like 'Feel the pain and rejection of being dumped – and date again anyway' or 'He's just not that into you' (the last one is a real title). Since I'm horribly judgemental about people based on their reading material, I'm careful not to fall on my own sword.

Reading material is also a great way of judging whether you could ever fancy a particular stranger on the train. A man reading Proust is trying too hard to be an intellectual, a man reading Dan Brown is not trying hard enough to be an intellectual and a man who's reading Terry Pratchett will force you to go to role-playing gaming evenings and may disturbingly want you to dress up as Princess Leia on occasion. I want a sexy, Nietzsche-reading superman.

Being able to read is a tremendous blessing and one that we probably overlook when we're thinking of things to be grateful for. Exercise this fabulous skill as often and as passionately as you can.

How did it go?

Q   I find reading really boring. What do you suggest?

A   How about magazines, journals or digests? Better still, how do you feel about comic books? Don't laugh, a lot of people I know learnt another language through reading comic books. Nowadays you have religious comic books, romantic ones, superhero ones, gothic ones – a vast array to choose from. Give it a try, you might like it.

Q   My boyfriend and I disagree on everything, especially what constitutes good literature. He tries to make me feel stupid and I hate that about him. How do I get him off his high horse?

A   I get the feeling you're not exactly a shy wallflower yourself so perhaps what's annoying you is more that he doesn't agree with you rather than that he's trying to make you feel stupid. On this one, you'll both have to agree to disagree as literature is a very personal taste and you should respect that.

Q   I read books that make me think 'I could have written that'. Do you think I should try?

A   Yes, definitely. Even if you decide not to present it for publication, writing can be tremendous fun and it's a good way to explore other lives.

24

Water works

From water meditations to finding out what's in your taps, water is life-affirming.

Water, water everywhere and so much more than drink! Let water play a main role in your life and you'll be left sparkling.

A walk through the woods for me is not complete until I hear the sound of a gurgling brook somewhere in the undergrowth. That is when the real magic begins. Have you ever run your hand in wild, cool water? Nothing in the world feels like it. It's like the tonic of life.

Now before you run off to the woods and start drinking from these random streams and brooks, please don't. Water may look pure but it has the ability to hide within it a multitude of sins and blessings. It contains trace metals and minerals, some of which can be good for you and some less so. So the more you know about the water you're drinking, the better. Ask your local water board for a report on the composition of the water in your tap. I bet you just thought it was H_2O. Oh no, there are all manner of bits and bobs in there to treat it so that it is fit for human consumption. They estimate that the water running through the taps in the average London household has passed through the human body about seven times. I don't give you that fact to gross you out, more to illustrate that water is a precious resource and when we turn on the tap, it's not connected to some pretty little woodland lake.

Bringing the energy of water into your life really helps soothe you emotionally. Try putting a regular visit to the swimming pool into your hectic schedule. The first couple of times it will seem like a real hassle with towels, bathing costumes and waxing of legs to consider but, once you get into a rhythm with it, you'll find that it relaxes you mentally and uplifts you emotionally – to say nothing of the physical benefits.

My favourite sort of water is holy water. Not just the Catholic sort but also water that is taken from holy wells all around the world. Just about every culture and religion has the presence of holy water. It is as if the ancients knew that we are comprised primarily of water and that water is the element most likely to allow us to take in divine blessings.

Here's an idea for you...

Energise your water with love! Before you cart me off to the funny farm, Dr Masaru Emoto found that the crystal structure of water changes if you direct love or hate towards it. Naturally we want loved-up water so write 'I love you' on a piece of paper and tape it to the outside of your water jug. Check if this makes you feel any better about the world than drinking 'uncharged' water from a tap.

A great and effective way of working with water is to put your negative thoughts into it and flush it away. You can do this in a couple of ways. Sit with a bowl of ordinary tap water in front of you and imagine a ball of light coming in through the crown of your head, forcing all negativity downwards before it. You can imagine the negativity as a sludgy dirt that moves downwards. Imagine it moving out of your belly button and down into the bowl of water in front of you. The shining ball of light then pops out of your belly button, leaving it all pristine. Take the bowl of imaginary negativity and flush it away. Even easier is to sleep with a glass of water on your bedside table each night and then flush it away in the morning.

I know that the suggestions above will be a little too woo-woo for some of you out there but if you believe in the mysteries of energy, you'll know that just about anything is possible. Even the great scientist Albert Einstein believed that we are all part of a whole and it is just the delusion of our consciousness that makes us believe we are separate from anything. Stick that in your test tube and smoke it – ha!

'Til taught by pain, men really know not what good water is worth.'
LORD BYRON, from *Don Juan*

Defining idea...

109

How did it go?

Q **I can't seem to be able to drink the two litres of water a day recommended. I always forget; any ideas?**

A *Did you know that herbal teas and cordials also count in your water drinking quota? I particularly love elderberry cordial and can easily drink a couple of glasses of it a day. Add to that a few mugs of peppermint tea and Bob's your uncle, you've drunk your quota. Try experimenting to see what suits you. Perhaps a slice of lemon and some ice?*

Q **I'd love to have some water and fish in my garden but the neighbourhood cats are always coming in and out. What should I do?**

A *Have a pond but don't keep fish. I've noticed that even with netting, the cats seem to get in and grab them. We've now had a pond for many years with a water feature but no fish. Strangely you do still get toads in the pond, no idea where they come from, but life will always seek out water so put in the pond and the wildlife will come of its own accord.*

Q **Is mineral water better than normal tap water?**

A *I prefer the taste as there is quite a bit of chlorine in our tap water. However, I never forget how lucky we are to have water that is safe to drink on tap and I always order tap water in restaurants as I think it's a rip-off there, with the mark-ups. In short, I'm sure mineral water is better on some levels but not so much so that you should forsake tap water.*

25

A change of scene

**From the countryside to the coast, a break is as much of
a necessity as food and a home.**

*Having two days away in a completely
different setting can make you feel much,
much happier with your daily round once you
return.*

Sometimes you can feel like a hamster on a wheel, doing the same things over and
over again. Getting up at the same time, going to the same shops, the same desk at
work and the same faces around you all the time. It can make you forget that you're
here to explore and enjoy life rather than wear down the pavement into a rut.
One of the best ways of countering this is to pick a place that is the direct opposite
of your usual abode. If you live in the country, book a couple of days in a bustling
city. Choose to visit during the week rather the weekend as restaurants and exhibi-
tions are less busy and there's simply nothing more relaxing than walking about
at a leisurely pace while all the busy-bee workers are frenetically going about their
weekday lives.

Here's an idea for you...

House sit or house swap with a friend. As the holiday season comes upon us many of our friends who live by the coast or in the city (if we're coastal dwellers) are off on holiday, leaving their homes empty. Ask if they want a house sitter and enjoy an almost free holiday. You'll be shopping for groceries in a new town, discovering new walks and maybe even looking after a dog (a pleasant experience if you're not allowed them in your city flat).

If, like me, you're a city girl then head for the country or the coast. The change of pace can be startling and sometimes people suffer from a 'communication neurosis' whereby they feel the need to have their laptops and mobiles on to feel connected with world. Here's an idea: make the only blackberries you see on your break the kind you put in jams. Or head to somewhere like the Brecon Beacons where mobile reception is usually pretty bad.

I regularly housesit for a friend of mine in Sussex. The days that I am off house-sitting near the seafront in Newhaven are heavenly. Early morning walks to the beach, lunch at a dockside pub, a stroll through flea markets and then back home to cook the fish I got first thing in the morning at the market off the harbour. As an urban-dweller, I find it amazing that I can go down to the dock and pick up a fish caught that day to cook in the evening. It seems almost unreal to see the catch all lined up on ice instead of covered in cellophane at the supermarket.

One of the big mistakes that people make is to save their money and time up and then blow a substantial amount of money on two weeks somewhere exotic. That's all fine and good, but imagine how much pressure you're putting on yourself to have a great holiday. You've saved up your days and your money for a big break and you expect the pay-off to be a great time, great weather and to come back feeling very rested. However, if the hotel isn't what you expected or the weather turns bad or you have a row with your boyfriend, you could well return stressed, cheated and miserable because it will be a whole year before you can afford another break.

'Live and see, move around and see more.'

Arab proverb

Defining idea...

A better idea is to spend little and often. The weekend break can be fantastic with a little planning. Spend a couple of weekends doing extra chores like washing or cleaning out the fridge so that on your weekend away, you're not thinking about housework or what you'll have to do before work on Monday. Before you leave for your break on the Friday, lay out and plan what you'll wear to work on the Monday. Turn off your mobile and give the number of the hotel you're staying in to a family member in case of emergencies. Don't even think about bringing your laptop. Let the office know that you are away for the weekend and so can't be contacted. Then enjoy exploring a completely new place with no worries beyond which restaurant to have dinner in.

How did it go?

Q   **I had a break at the coast and I loved it so much, I want to move there. How can I make my dream a reality?**

A   *Me too! I love the coast and would love to live there. My plan for making my dream come true is to save, plot and scheme. I know that working in London for the next five years will give me enough in savings and contacts to be able to start a satellite career more or less anywhere in the world. So that's what I'll do. I am plotting my escape route and so should you, and then, whenever you feel disheartened and tired with your game plan, take another short trip to the coast to remind yourself of what it is you're working towards.*

Q   **I'm much too busy to take a break right now. How can I possibly go off to the country or seaside when I have a million deadlines on my head?**

A   *They say nobody ever says on their death bed, 'I wish I'd worked more'. Deadlines will always be there, work will always be there. This was brought home to me one time when I suddenly and inexplicably got very, very sick right on deadline for the magazine I worked for. The editor I worked for was brilliant and had had plan Bs for every feature I'd been working on. He simply replaced what was going in and told me to get better. I was partly upset that the world didn't fall apart when I wasn't able to be there but mostly I was relieved that I could concentrate on getting better. Take a break, the world won't end.*

26

Love not war

Fighting with your partner can cause you a lot of pain and misery; learn how to stop.

Being right isn't as important as being loving so put down your cudgel and find a flower to throw instead.

Most healthy relationships have ups and downs and sometimes you have to fight your corner. If your girlfriend gets insanely jealous every time you even speak to another girl, you have a problem. If your boyfriend refuses to be seen out in public with you and wants you to keep your relationship secret, you have a problem. If your boyfriend thinks he prefers your brother to you, you definitely have a problem. The point is that there are some situations that are deal-breakers but the rest is about compromise, compromise, compromise.

The best way to learn to compromise is to step into your partner's shoes. Don't do this literally as heels quickly lose their shape and you can trip up in big boots. Do it by thinking for a minute about how the situation looks from his or her viewpoint. Imagine for a second that you're your boyfriend's lawyer and you have to make a case for his side of the argument. What were his motives for doing what he did or

The next time you have a fight with your partner, write them a letter. You don't have to send it (in fact you probably shouldn't), you don't even have to read it back to yourself but write all your feelings down on paper anyway. This should dissipate some of the rage you might be feeling. Once you've expressed all your feelings of anger and righteousness, take a fresh piece of paper and write a love note to your partner that only says what you like about them. Send that one.

saying what he said? It may seem a bit of a convoluted and strange exercise but really try to imagine how you'd argue his case. Not your case. His case.

Oftentimes you'll find that the reason people do and say hurtful things is not because they're being malicious but because they can't see how they're hurting you. So, instead of fighting as though you were faced with an adversary, you should try to honestly express what you're feeling and – this is very important – say explicitly what they can do or say to make it better.

Here's an example. Suppose you have a row that starts because you feel cold and your husband feels hot. You see his refusal to turn on the heating as evidence of him not caring for you. He, for his part, doesn't see why you can't just put on more clothing, given that he would feel extra hot if the heating was on. Perhaps he thinks you don't care about his comfort either. Something small like this can quickly escalate into a horrible argument where both of you are convinced that the other person is in the wrong. A good way to deal with it would be for you to say 'I feel like you don't care about me when you refuse to turn the heating on. I need reassurance in the form of a warming cuddle that this isn't the case.' At this point your husband will look at you as if you've gone crazy.

You'll have two choices in front of you then. You can either return to argument mode or you can laugh and go fetch a cardigan or blanket to warm yourself up in. The first choice is a quick way to ruin your mood and your evening. The second choice will probably result in your husband also laughing and turning the heating on, even if he has to sit around in Bermuda shorts to cope.

'Make sure you never, never argue at night. You just lose a good night's sleep, and you can't settle anything until morning anyway.'
ROSE KENNEDY, Matriarch of the famous Kennedy political dynasty

Defining idea...

The way to steer yourself out of an attitude of anger and resentment is to treat your partner with the same compassion you'd show for someone with whom you weren't in a relationship. I mean, think about it; if a friend of yours was visiting and had issues with the temperature of your home, would you insist she just put up with it? Probably not, as a good host you'd check she was OK and make adjustments to make her as comfortable as possible. Why do we think that it's OK to not have the same consideration for our partners?

How did it go?

Q   **I try biting my tongue when my husband says something annoying but we still end up arguing. How can we stop doing it?**

A   *Biting your tongue is no answer as you'll only end up storing up resentment for later. Much better out than in. However, tact and a calm delivery is a much better way of saying something than yelling. I once said some pretty unforgivable things in the heat of the moment to an ex-boyfriend. The silly thing is that they were all true and if I had said it in a calm manner, he'd probably have agreed with me.*

Q   **My best friend says that she has never met anyone as obnoxious as my boyfriend and suggests I dump him. Should I, just on her say-so?**

A   *Obviously not as you've hinted with 'just on her say-so'. After all, your best friend may not have a wide enough experience to judge the truly obnoxious. Has she hung out with rock stars and pubescent teenagers? If not, she can't say categorically that your boyfriend is the worst. However, she probably does have your best interests at heart so you should consider her comments closely.*

Q   **My girlfriend gives me the silent treatment whenever we argue. How do I get her to speak to me?**

A   *Not speaking is probably the worst form of row there is as there is no comeback to it. Try playing her at her own game and staying silent too. I guarantee it will drive her insane enough to start negotiations. If not, you'll both eventually forget what you were rowing about. One hopes.*

27

Child's play

Children can teach us a lot about how to live a happy life – even when they're being snotty-nosed brats.

When you seem to hit a block acting like a grown-up, it's time to get back to basics and remember how to act like the big kid you really are.

Try to think back to what you were like as a child. Were you quiet or rowdy? Well-behaved or naughty? Did you do something memorable like win a competition or set fire to the kitchen (sorry about that, Mum)? Do you have any siblings? Did you get along with them? Thinking back to that time, you'll have a number of memories that come up according to your own individual experience but one memory that is likely to be common to most people is how rarely adults listen to kids.

Children are often ignored and I recall once saying 'Mum? Mum? Mum?' about 50 times before finally Ma yelled 'WHAT?' It was impossible to get an adult's undivided attention, truly impossible. Now it may surprise you but this is still happening to you, right now, even as you stand there a fully-fledged adult. You have an inner child that is probably rather used to being ignored.

Here's an idea for you...

Think of a game you enjoyed playing as a child, be it scrabble or monopoly or even hopscotch. Then... yes, you've guessed it... have a go! Rope in a playmate and enjoy a trip back to childhood. You'll be surprised at how much fun a game you haven't played since childhood can be. It'll rejuvenate you more than any wrinkle cream.

In the Hawaiian spiritual tradition called Huna, there are three basic selves (there are other selves too but let's not complicate things here): your child self, your conscious self and your higher self. Your child self controls your carnal desires and wants and is also in charge of your body; your conscious self looks after the thinking and reasoning bits and your higher self is your connection to divinity.

You don't have to believe in Huna or in the existence of a child self within you but it can't hurt to keep an open mind, especially if you regularly suffer from poor health or are prone to accidents. Since this child self controls the body, he or she may just be trying to get your attention. A classic case of this is the man who books a holiday after a long, long time and is really looking forward to it but a lucrative bit of work crops up right at the time of the holiday and the holiday is cancelled. The day the man was meant to go on holiday, he gets horrible flu-like symptoms and can't work either. This is because if you promise your body a break and then renege on it without a compromise with your child self, that part of you is within its rights (and abilities) to force a break upon you. This may be petulant and immature but the hint of what this self is like is in the name.

It is also beneficial to listen to real-life children too. Two years ago I was suffering from a broken heart and my sister, being a kindly sort, decided a spot of babysitting would sort me right out. She handed over my niece and nephew and beat a hasty retreat out the door. My nephew, at that time, was six years old. He is a happy little boy who is easily distracted. He is perfection. Both the children could sense my unhappiness and, instead of being their usual feral selves, they sprawled on top of me in a heap and gave me a hug. 'Hassan,' I said, cuddling him. 'Tell me the secret to happiness. You're always happy.' 'OK, but it's a secret so only you can hear.' He made his little sister block her ears and then he leant in and whispered in my ear. 'Eat lots of sugar. Move around a lot. And read funny stories.' That is probably the best advice I have ever had in my life.

'Adults are always asking little kids what they want to be when they grow up because they're looking for ideas.'
PAULA POUNDSTONE, American comic

Defining idea...

How did it go?

Q   **I am not comfortable in the company of children and I can't remember what it was like being a child – any tips on how to get back there?**

A   *Smell is very evocative. From certain baking smells to baby powder or the smell of rusks, there are a number of smells that can transport you right back to your own childhood. Why not go on an olfactory tour and try and find a smell that makes you nostalgic?*

Q   **My children don't induce feelings of peace and calm in me as they can be little terrors – what exactly can I learn from their attempts to destroy everything as quickly and loudly as possible?**

A   *Abandonment; you can learn freedom! Why don't you tear through the house one morning yelling and skidding into rooms and jumping on the sofa? They will freeze in terror that they've finally managed to drive Mum dotty and you will enjoy surprising them and yourself. Of course the stunned silence won't last but it'll be an interesting break from yelling at them to stop.*

Q   **I had a very unhappy childhood. Why would I want to go back there?**

A   *It's even more important for you to regress to a child-like state as you will be re-making your childhood into a happy one. You don't have to live in the past but nurture your inner child in some way; was there a doll you always wanted when you were little but couldn't have? Buy it for yourself and brush her hair, make pretty clothes for her, do something a little childish. It's OK now, you're an adult and you can look after yourself.*

28

Clever, not cheap

When society pressurises you to spend, spend, spend, gain the confidence to just say no.

Frugality doesn't need to turn you into a joyless cheapskate. Get financially savvy and no longer dread the dull thud of your credit card bill on the mat.

How much money do you have in your purse or pocket? Those who respect money could probably tell you almost to the penny how much they have. Those, like me, who have a more complicated relationship with it, will probably get it quite wrong. The problem with money is that it is rarely what it truly is: simply a medium of exchange. No, money is often a way of expressing your beliefs about your status, class and even worth as a human being. Your attitude to money can enslave you or set you free.

Economical living can make you feel deprived and miserable or it can fill you with a sense of achievement and excitement. Take the task of living well within your means as an enjoyable challenge rather than something to be feared or resented.

Here's an idea for you...

Challenge yourself to find, make or acquire very cheaply a present for a friend whose birthday is coming up. The rule is that your friend must love the gift and you can't spend more than a fiver on it. Funnily enough the secret to doing this one well is to listen to your friends carefully as we often learn about their preferences through careful listening. My friend once made me bergamot bath salts as I had mentioned in two separate conversations my love of bergamot and of baths.

First things first: make your monthly budget. List your income and your expenditure and see what you have got left each month to play with. For the first couple of days of the month, don't buy anything; just keep some money in your pocket. If you're a spendaholic, this will be quite difficult but try to see how liberating it is to have money you could spend if you wanted to but then not spend it. The decision is yours and you don't have to bow to pressure to buy.

Clothes can be a heavy expenditure, especially if you need to look smart for work. Since retro clothing became more popular, more and more people are hunting out second-hand and vintage shops to stock up on bygone fashions. This is great for the wardrobe and for the pocket as you can really pick up some superb bargains. Avoid the dedicated vintage stores as they overprice and look for second-hand/charity shops in areas with an older population as they are more likely to donate originals that will be in excellent condition. I once found a gorgeous Biba coat for just £3. You will get a frisson of excitement at finding a designer item at a fraction of the cost.

Another major expense is the monthly grocery shopping bill. Take a look at where you can make savings. Have you tried some of the supermarket generic brands for taste and quality? Some things you'll find are awful but a lot of others are very good and a fraction of the price of big name brands. Start gently and try substituting something you always buy like washing powder or pasta with a supermarket own brand and see if your family notice the difference. If not, then swap to it and save loads of wonga.

'I've been rich and I've been poor. Believe me, rich is better.'

MAE WEST, actress and wit

Defining idea...

Get your family and friends in on the act and share tips for saving money and still living well. Perhaps you can revert to barter for some things? If your cousin is great at gardening and you're brilliant at dress-making, barter and use your respective skills to help each other out. You'll save money and have the satisfaction of a job well done.

During the Second World War, pamphlets were distributed to housewives encouraging them to 'make do and mend'. This meant that when clothing got worn, they'd be mended rather than chucked out. Leftovers were made into fresh meals. Very little was thrown away. While we're now in a period of rampant consumerism, there is a quiet revolution happening, led by those who can see the logic of a 'waste not, want not' attitude. It is a simpler, happier way of living that contributes significantly to a sense of inner peace.

How did it go?

Q   If I'm making the payments on my credit bills each month, why shouldn't I splurge out on nice things?

A   *No reason at all but can I ask you, when was the last time you saved up for something? Instant gratification may seem wonderful but it slowly chips away at your sense of anticipation, excitement and how much you value things. See if saving instead of splurging feels as good.*

Q   My friends are all in better-paid jobs than me and I don't have the money for the posh dinners they tend to go for. How can I still see them?

A   *Me too, most of my pals are rich and I'm definitely not. Why don't you have a picnic in the summer where you each bring some goodies along and head to a nice park to relax in the sunshine? In the winter, you could invite your friends around for a mulled wine and mince pies evening. This is relatively inexpensive and cheerful. Be honest with your mates as to what you can afford. They will understand or they're not true friends.*

Q   My debts are so crippling that I barely have enough to even economise each month – what should I do?

A   *Contact your local Citizen's Advice Bureau to get some information on what you can do about this. You could also call the Consumer Credit Counselling Service (www.cccs.co.uk), a charity who will give you independent advice after working through your budget and how much you owe. Don't, whatever you do, consolidate your debt as you'll only be trapped in the same situation for longer.*

29

Advertising is evil

**Logos, posters, labels; we are drowning in advertising.
Learn how to fight back.**

Yell 'I am not a consumer, I am a free man!'
and see if you can't beat the advertisers
at their own game.

Obviously all advertising isn't evil as we need some advertising to find out what's happening in the world. An advertisement for a concert we want to see is the very opposite of evil as it gives us the means to go and have a moving experience. If you are promoting a product or an experience, you need to be able to communicate with your audience to ensure it is a success. I appreciate that and I'm not calling for a ban on all advertising.

The problem is not with an unobtrusive poster or a billboard; it's with the sneaky ways that advertising tries to get in on every aspect of human endeavour. Sports events are sponsored by companies who flash their logos over everything, including the players. TV advertisements force us to watch if we don't want to miss the next bit of our TV show. Cinema audiences are forced to sit through adverts instead of

Here's an idea for you...

Pick out all the labels from your clothes. Not only will they hang better and you'll have no itching around the neck or back, you will also not have to see a brand name each time you get dressed. You already paid for your clothes; why should you have to give the company free subliminal advertising to you each time you get dressed?

just trailers at the cinema now. The advertisers are now even trying desperately to find a way to use the popularity of social networking websites to their advantage.

None of this would be very sinister if it didn't work. No advertiser would bother us if he thought his adverts were falling on deaf ears. No, the reason advertising has gone crazy is that it works. American economist, Juliet Schor, estimated almost a decade ago that the average American's annual spend is increased by $200 for every hour of TV (above the national average) he or she watches each week.

Ads make us more stressed because they constantly assault us on subconscious and conscious levels. They are a constant visual 'noise' that we simply can't shut up, no matter how hard we try. Our daily commute is plastered with poster ads and even digital moving ads on buses and some billboards. We are constantly taking in that there are millions of products out there for us to consume. It is spiritually and physically draining.

It is pretty hard to avoid TV ads (though several people I know lead very happy lives without a TV) but there are other ways you can strike back at the corrosive influence of advertising in your life. Try to get rid of branded packs of things in your home. So buy un-branded ceramic containers for things like flour, sugar, coffee, etc. Unfortunately we seem to be swamped with packaging nowadays – very useful for the advertiser who wants to stick their logo right where you can see it as much as possible – and the days of things wrapped in plain paper are long gone. However, you can return to a slower pace of life by getting rid of a lot of packaging and storing things in pretty, air-tight containers.

'History will see advertising as one of the real evil things of our time. It is stimulating people constantly to want things, want this, want that.'
MALCOLM MUGGERIDGE, journalist and broadcaster

Defining idea...

The next act of anti-advertising you can do is to ensure you tick the right box on forms to avoid direct mail advertising. You know all that junk mail that gets through anyway? How about writing 'Take me off your mailing list,' onto their order forms and posting it back to them using the pre-paid envelope they provide. This costs you nothing and should start to get your message across to them. You can also contact the mailing preference service to be removed from the mailing lists companies buy in (www.mpsonline.org.uk). It is now not uncommon for marketing, aka advertising calls, to come to your home on a Sunday. My dad usually yells at them but I saw a brilliant wind-up whereby the person being called pretended he was an inspector at the scene of a crime and that the telemarketer was under suspicion of murder because he called at that number. Probably going a bit far but a good indication of what you can do with a little imagination.

How did it go?

Q I work in advertising – are you calling me evil?

A   *Yes. OK, no, not really but you must admit that all those brainstorming ses-sions where you think of more ingenious ways to get people to buy things they don't need or want are a bit soul-destroying. Surely all that knowl-edge of human psychology and behaviour could be put to better use? Just a thought.*

Q Your suggestions will cost a lot of money that I don't have and isn't that just more consumerism?

A   *My suggestion to get storage for everyday items shouldn't cost you much if you find your things as bargain buys in car boot sales or charity shops. It can also be huge fun trawling through bits of junk to find your perfect treasure.*

Q I get really influenced by make-up and perfume ads. How can I stop the impulse to buy?

A   *It may be that it's the beautiful images of the perfect girls that you're attracted by and not the product itself. After all, don't you feel disap-pointed sometimes once you've got it home? Try making a scrapbook of image ideas that contain the adverts of those pretty girls but use it as a resource to inspire different looks, achievable with your existing make-up. You can still buy the occasional bit of new product, just be sure to clear out one item of old make-up from your bag to ensure that you're not just stock-piling.*

30

Two for tea

When was the last time you invited one of your closest friends over for tea or a couple of beers? Discover the pleasure in simple one-on-ones.

Social gatherings with lots of your friends around are fantastic but there's something magical in giving one of your friends your complete attention.

Friendships need to be nurtured in order to grow. We assume that the occasional 'poke' on Facebook or a hurried text is enough to let our friends know that we are thinking of them but it isn't enough to sustain an intimate relationship. There is an uppermost limit of people you can comfortably know and interact with (scientist Robin Dunbar placed the number as 150) and our relationships will change over time so that some people drop out of our lives while others come in. Those that you choose to be friends with are precious and deserve some one-on-one time with you.

Here's an idea for you...

When you next invite a friend round for a simple party for two, make a bit of an effort. Get out the good china, make a particularly elaborate dish, chill a bottle of bubbly. In short, do everything you'd do for a posh dinner party but lavish it on your one mate instead. Your friend will feel special and you'll feel decadent.

We are often reticent about sharing personal information on the phone with friends; you need that person there in front of you in order to bare your heart. Make an extra-special effort to contact a friend who you suspect might be going through a rough time, perhaps a break-up or an illness? It's often those times that people think we want to be alone with our misery that we'd love to be taken out and away from it all. Get your psychic radar working overtime to identify those who need a friendly chat most.

Life changes can also change you; your personality, your views and even your physical appearance. This means that you should often touch base with your friends to re-acquaint yourselves with each other and ensure that your friendship isn't suffering from being strangers to each other in the here and now. Some friends from university are now so different that it is as if they were different people back then. And they were. They were teenagers, setting out into the big, bad world and now they're adults who've been out there some time and may have families of their own.

This doesn't mean you can't still remain friends and reminisce about times gone by but you should also make allowances for changes in temperament. It's very sad when friends grow apart due to an inflexible notion of what the other is like. One of my best friends is an actress and, as her success grew, we grew further and further apart. Quite apart from the physical distance of living in different countries, I felt we were growing apart because she had changed (I felt that the film world had changed her and made her more fake). My mother then pointed out that she had not changed at all, that she'd always been a bit of a luvvie, and that what had changed was that I was much more intolerant of any perceived insincerity. She hadn't changed, I had. Once I came to this realisation, I stopped being snappy with my friend and started to remember all the fantastic things about her. After all, if she could put up with me changing, surely I could put up with her being 'diplomatic' with the truth at times?

'Think where man's glory most begins and ends, And say my glory was I had such friends.'

W. B. YEATS

Defining idea...

One word about secrets; if you up the number of times you meet your friends for one-on-one dates, you'll find that a lot of secrets come up – sometimes concerning other friends. Some people have personalities that make them perfect gossips while others can remain perfectly tight-lipped. If you plan to ever be anyone's confidante, you must suppress any tendency toward gossip you may have. It is a privilege to be given a secret to keep and you should consider them to be as priceless jewels given over to you for safe-keeping. Look after them and you'll soon be known as a true friend.

How did
it go?

Q **I don't have any really close friends, more groups of friends –
how do I invite just one person without offending the others in
that group?**

A *If there's someone you particularly like in your group of friends, do it
anyway. People are normally too busy to be offended and it's not as if
you're inviting a group of people round to yours and leaving one person
out. The group will cope if only one of them has been invited.*

Q **My best friend and I often have tea together so how do I make it
special?**

A *How about getting some special cakes from a patisserie? Or baking some
cup cakes and decorating them elaborately? You can also vary the things
you do together so perhaps book a visiting manicurist and get your nails
done while you chat or go to a coffee shop instead of having tea at home
for a change of scenery. Make an effort to do different things and it will
feel very special.*

Q **I have a young child and so a heart-to-heart is a little difficult.
Should I still invite my friend over?**

A *Yes! Try to time it with Junior's nap but, even if you can't, your friend will
understand that you can't give her all your attention. If the weather is nice,
have your tea party in the garden so your little one can run around and
you can all relax. If you're really worried, consider getting a babysitter for a
couple of hours. You'll still be at home so you won't be worried or rushing
to the phone to check everything's OK.*

31

Say a little prayer

Even if you're an atheist, prayer is a proven way to tap into the power of human hope.

Prayer doesn't have to be ritualised; find a way of connecting with something greater than you and you'll feel a great sense of comfort.

I have a prayer list. This is a list of people I pray for each night in order to get them happiness, health and a general sense of well-being. This would be surprising to a lot of my friends if they knew about it as I'm the least likely person to have a prayer recipient list. In fact I've often vocalised my irritation at people who insist upon praying for others when they haven't actually asked for it. I find it intrusive, presumptuous and frankly a little weird. I don't want spiritual interlopers between me and my deities of choice.

Here's an idea for you...

Each day put a few coppers in a jar, maybe some silver on days you're feeling flush. When the jar is full, take it all down to your favourite charity and donate it. Then start again. This daily practice gives you a sense of grace as, when you donate it, you'll be answering someone else's prayers somewhere.

However, the difference between me and the prayer fascists is that I don't tell the person I'm praying for that I'm doing – at least not unless they specifically and unbidden by me ask me to. I just do it because I know it works and the person recovering due to a bout of prayer doesn't need to know where their recovery comes from.

There have been a number of scientific studies into the power of prayer. One of the most famous was a double blind study that was conducted at the San Francisco General Hospital's Coronary Care Unit in the 1980s. Patients were selected at random by a computer to receive prayer from a group of individuals as well as additional prayer from folks not connected to the study. The patients, doctors and even the scientist conducting the study were not told which had been selected. They found that the group selected for prayer, in comparison to the control group, had much better health, needed less medication or resuscitation and suffered far fewer deaths. This was true whether or not the recipient believed in God or not.

Some scientists believe that it is the sense of being in a community that cares about you that causes prayer to be so healing. Indeed in the shamanic tradition, there is a group healing that is sometimes done when one person really needs a massive amount of healing for something serious. A group of shamans will 'journey' to bring back healing for the person in question. I have had such a healing and, while you don't need to do anything, you feel a tremendous sense of love and care emanating towards you and that's really very powerful. It makes you feel held and comforted and is a real lift to the spirit. However, this doesn't explain why prayer also works when the person being prayed for has no idea this is being done for them.

'Prayer must never be answered; if it is, it ceases to be prayer and becomes correspondence.'

OSCAR WILDE

Defining idea...

An atheist researcher was of the opinion that prayer works like a placebo on people but the problem with that is that the patients did not know that they were being prayed for and some studies have even been done on fungi in Petri dishes that definitely couldn't believe in the placebo effect. Yet the fungi that were prayed for flourished far more than control group fungi. It has worked for seeds and micro-organisms as well so there's definitely something there.

Why don't you make a list of people in your circle or community that may need the boost a spot of being prayed for could give them? Having produced this list, pray for the people on it in any way that makes you feel comfortable. This may be within a certain religious tradition or it could just be lighting a candle and meditating in front of it while thinking of the outcomes you'd like to achieve for the folks on your prayer list. Give it a go, you can't really do any harm and you may end up doing a world of good.

How did it go?

Q   **I am an atheist and this idea doesn't sit well with me. Who exactly am I praying to?**

A   *You don't have to believe in God to believe in transcendental states. A really fabulous meal or a beautiful piece of music can transport you to a higher state and those don't have much to do with any deity. Experiment, take what you enjoy and leave what you can't stomach. You're not required to believe in any God in order to show concern for your fellow man and send him some healing thoughts.*

Q   **I feel like my prayers are never answered – what am I doing wrong?**

A   *Prayers are a way of spreading blessings around, they don't work in the same way as a shopping list. You can't ask for certain outcomes, give a deadline and then wonder why you haven't had the result you asked for. You have to trust that, having said your peace, your prayer is not in vain. That's the faith part of the equation.*

Q   **My sister says that I should pray in the manner of our own faith but I feel happier just lighting a candle and saying my prayer without any ritual. How can I get her off my back?**

A   *Avoid the conversation. You don't need to rub her nose in your beliefs and you shouldn't let her rub yours in hers. Just relax and offer to make her a cup of tea if she starts up on the subject. You can easily keep changing the subject till she gets the message. And if she doesn't, explicitly tell her to butt out of your personal spiritual life as it's nothing to do with her. Sometimes you have to be blunt.*

32

Picture perfect

Cull the bad photos and bad memories from your life by creating albums of eternal joy.

A photo's worth a thousand words so make sure you have some chatterbox albums to browse through on rainy days or for when you need inspiration.

Have you ever seen professional tourists? I mean the sort of tourists who make touring an art. They take photos like they mean it; everything is photographed but it is also interestingly photographed so they'll take distance pics that look like they're leaning on the Tower of Pisa or they'll get on the floor to take pics of their family under giant spiders, like the one by Louise Bourgeois outside the Tate Modern. In short, they get excited about producing really interesting photos for their albums. If, like me, you're too busy enjoying the moment to take a photo of it, here's a thought to make you remember. When you're old and perhaps can't travel as easily as before, you can revisit feelings, thoughts and the excitement by looking at old photographs. They are also one of the greatest treasures you can leave your future generations of family.

Here's an idea for you...

Scrapbooking is a massive craze in the States and it's fast catching on in Britain. The idea is to make picture books with photos, card and creativity. You can stick memos to remind you where you were when a particular photo was taken. For example, you can stick in things like 'baby's first booty' or your baby's hospital wristband if it is a baby scrapbook you're making. Or perhaps a Valentine's card from your beloved if you're making a romantic scrapbook.

Looking at old photographs of my family, I'm amazed at the stories they tell. I have one of my grandmother in very dapper 1940s wide leg trousers, with an English short jacket and a sun hat on, looking young and elegant and not at all like her older, rather forbidding self, always in a traditional sari. This photo reminds me that people we think of as 'old' were young once and probably made a much more exciting job of it than we're doing now. It is only through beautiful photos like these that we get a sense of the person as an individual rather than just as the relationship we have with them.

In your own photo collection there will be some photos that just make you smile and mean so much to you. Where have you got them? Languishing in the back of a drawer, in an old cellophane album or in some dusty box in the attic? Take out your best photos and frame them or put them in a lovely tissue separated album to preserve them properly. I once found a gorgeous photo of my friend Ross as a child. He had the exact same grumpy look on his face that he sometimes has now. It made me laugh. Instead of having it where it could be seen, he had it in a kitchen drawer where it was being spattered with coffee and whatnot. I had it framed while he was away on holiday and when he returned it made him laugh too as he hadn't seen it in ages. Apparently the grumpy look was because a girl had just tried to kiss him and we all know that girls are horrible and snotty.

'Most things in life are moments of pleasure and a lifetime of embarrassment; photography is a moment of embarrassment and a lifetime of pleasure.'
TONY BENN, British politician

Defining idea...

What hidden treasures do you have in your drawers? Take a look today and bring them out into the open for you and your family to enjoy. In this age of digital photography we suffer from rarely bothering to go and get proper prints made of photos but you should try and get extra-special photos made into paper memories as well as on some disc.

However, one of the benefits of digital photos is that we're much more likely to delete a bad photo from the memory card but, for some reason, we hang on to bad photos in our print envelopes. Perhaps we feel that a bit of the soul has been captured in a photo and we don't want to throw that piece away? Whatever the reason, you enhance the power of good photos by culling the bad ones from your life. Start today and ruthlessly get rid of anything that is poorly shot or out of focus. You can also destroy any that remind you of miserable situations. Life's too short to dwell on celluloid memories of the bad times.

How did it go?

Q **My brother has taken all our family photos – how can I get him to give me some of these important photos?**

A *Ask him to meet you in town with them. Then beat him up and take them off him. OK, no, just seeing if you're paying attention. Take him along with you to a photo studio and get copies made while you wait. That way he doesn't have to let them out of his sight and you get your copies.*

Q **I can't bear the photos of me and my ex-husband. Is it OK to destroy them?**

A *That depends. If you have children, I would recommend that you don't as your children will want to see the relationship they came from documented. If you don't have children, it's up to you but I personally hold on to my history as it will be interesting to look back when I'm a little old lady and am no longer wanting to kill my ex. Much.*

Q **My ex has some dodgy photos of me and he refuses to send them back. It's really stressing me out – what should I do?**

A *Chill out. What's the worst that could happen? He sells them to a porn magazine? And? No matter how gorgeous you are, you're unlikely to generate the same level of interest as Pamela Anderson or Paris Hilton. I expect your ex is fine and wouldn't do anything indiscreet with them but is enjoying winding you up by pretending he would. Act as if you don't care and you soon genuinely won't.*

33
Church on Tuesday

Holy places can give you comfort irrespective of whether you believe in the faith to which they were built. Find a quiet time to sit and stare.

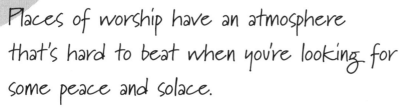
Places of worship have an atmosphere that's hard to beat when you're looking for some peace and solace.

A friend of mine always starts humming the theme from the film *Omen* whenever she sees a cathedral. For her the connotations of a place of worship like that are little boys intent on bringing forth the reign of Satan. However, for me, chilling Latin chants are the last thing going through my head when I see a cathedral. I am not Catholic but I remember asking my parents if I could convert when I was a child because, well, I liked the nuns' outfits and I loved the feeling of cool comfort inside a cathedral. I liked the fact that anyone, of any faith, could come and sit a while and contemplate whatever they wanted to contemplate. Traditionally that may have been God but nowadays it could be anything that gives you pause to think. Occasionally it will be the building itself that gives you pause to think. The Sacre Coeur (Sacred Heart) in Paris was my favourite until this year when I stumbled upon the Notre Dame (Our Lady) in Reims. Walking down a sidestreet, you suddenly come upon this huge, beautiful, gothic cathedral with some of the most stunning stained glass windows and carvings I have ever seen. It was breathtaking and my jaw hit the ground.

Most religions have a number of holy places and usually have a holiest of holies too. These are usually protected by a lot of ritual and rules and regulations. However, what some people don't realise is that you can create your own secular holy places. Think about a place where you last felt most inspired by the beauty around you. This may have been at a beach or a particularly perfect seat by the fire in a local pub or, more traditionally, a temple or church with all the bells and whistles. The point is not what your holy place is but more the feelings it evokes.

Make a commitment to yourself to visit your holy place at least once a fortnight to just sit and relax for a while. If this is not practical; for example, if your chosen holy place is in the Outer Hebrides and you live in Sussex, then make the visit once a year as a pilgrimage of sorts. When you get there, don't rush to be 'doing' stuff. You don't have to rush to light a candle and kneel in prayer as soon as you get in there. We are so caught up in the 'doing' culture that we forget that we can just be and that this is sometimes when we have the most powerful sacred experience.

Here's an idea for you... **This week visit a holy place at an awkward time when no-one is likely to be there. Go in between services to a church or visit a temple at about 9.30 when the early morning worshippers will have gone. You don't need to know what to do, just sit and relax, watching your breath coming in and going out. If religious holy places make you nervous, try visiting a beautiful natural spot or a building you think is architecturally gorgeous.**

There are those who say that the Earth is a sentient organism itself and I like to think that holy sites are the acupressure points on the Earth's body; places of energy where you can get a jolt of well-being simply by standing on them for a time. Many people use ley lines (lines of energy that criss-cross the surface of the Earth) to find these 'points of power' but I just use my intuition and I'd recommend you do as well. Once you've found your place of worship, don't let anyone talk you out of the feelings of happiness it gives you. Admittedly it will be pretty hard convincing your mother that a trip to your local pub is a moving sacred experience, nay, a pilgrimage of sorts, but give it a go anyway – just to see her face.

'I love you when you bow in your mosque, kneel in your temple, pray in your church. For you and I are sons of one religion and it is the spirit.'
KAHLIL GIBRAN, philosopher and poet

Defining idea...

149

How did it go?

Q **I'd love to visit a Hindu temple but I'm afraid of doing something wrong and offending somebody. What are the rules?**

A *If you're nervous about it, why not call up a temple local to you and ask the priests for advice as to appropriate dress and behaviour? Alternatively, be brave, and just turn up. Somebody is bound to point you in the right direction and most places of worship are very welcoming to respectful visitors.*

Q **Isn't it a bit weird to visit a church during the week? Won't the priest assume I'm hyper-religious and try and get me to volunteer for stuff?**

A *Maybe, but that's the great thing about volunteering – you get to decide if you want to do it or not. Don't let your fear of being roped into stuff deprive you of the beauty and stillness of places of worship.*

Q **I had a terrific time doing this idea; any more where that came from?**

A *How about doing a denominational retreat? Many contemplative orders of monks in a variety of different traditions allow secular visitors to join them for short retreats. You eat, work and sleep in exactly the same circumstances as the monks and you get plenty of time to relax and think about life, the universe and everything. Get a copy of the Good Retreat Guide to see what's out there.*

34

Signs and omens

Is someone trying to tell you something? What to look out for in your quest for meaning.

Signs and omens can be found in the strangest of places and, for those who know how to read them, they can be startlingly accurate.

Have you ever heard that rhyme about magpies and crows? One version goes like this:

One for sorrow
Two for mirth
Three for marriage
Four for a birth
Five for silver
Six for gold
Seven for a secret never to be told
Eight for heaven
Nine for hell
And for the Devil's very own self

Here's an idea for you... **Watch the behaviour of the birds around you and note anything unusual like a bird you don't normally see or strange interaction between two birds. Read up on what omens those birds represent (*The Secret Language of Birds* by Adele Nozedar is particularly brilliant). Even your common or garden birds had meanings for the ancients so your friendly local sparrow may very well have a message for you.**

The rhyme was originally about magpies and then changed to being about crows after the colonisation of America. It is about what spotting a certain number of the birds signifies. If you're anything like me, you'll chase that solitary magpie all over the place until you see another one. If you don't have that sort of time on your hands, you'd be well-advised to discount the whole notion as superstitious nonsense.

The thing about signs and portents is that in the past they tended to be made up for things that were rather unpleasant like death because without the aid of modern medicine it was always a bit of a lottery as to whether people would survive illnesses or accidents. There was also the uncertainty around harvests and the danger of being robbed whilst travelling. In short, life was a bit of a dangerous undertaking and so these signs were sought as a way of bringing some certainty into our lives.

Nowadays we don't need to signs for certainty but we can look out for them as a calling card from the universe, telling us that there are more mysterious phenomena to unlock out there. Given the ancient origins of looking for signs, many traditional ideas about what something means is rooted in nature.

In order to start being able to look for signs, you have to first re-attune yourself to your intuition. We often start ignoring our intuition, believing that logic is the best way to deal with any situation. It sometimes isn't. Here's an example: I often socialise in town during the week and I usually try to make it home at a reasonable hour. Occasionally it will get very late and I'll get a cab home. Once or twice I've walked home when it's very late, much to my mother's horror. However, the reason I can do that is one day, at a very bright and light 7pm, I caught a cab all the way home from town. I have no idea what made me do it but I wasn't going to get public transport and then walk home. I just wouldn't do it. The next day I found out that just outside the tube station at the time I'd have been coming home, someone got stabbed to death and a couple of witnesses were threatened. My mysterious insistence on a cab at a time that was unusual for me had saved me from a horrible situation.

'There are no unnatural or supernatural phenomena, only very large gaps in our knowledge of what is natural...we should strive to full those gaps of ignorance.'
EDGAR D. MITCHELL, Apollo 14 Astronaut

Defining idea...

When your intuition is on form, you will often see signs that alert you to what's going on. This can sometimes be in your dreams or it can be in nature. There are too many traditional associations to repeat here but, as an example, say you're out and about and you see a big black dog. How you interpret that sighting will depend on what you associate with dogs. If you see dogs as threatening, you may interpret that as a threat at work from an overbearing boss or colleague. If you see dogs as loyal then you may see that as help from an outside source in some aspect of your life. I once met a man who was so good at divination that he gave me the sighting of a black dog as a marker for when a particular thing was going to happen in my life. The day I spotted a black dog, lo and behold, that thing came to pass. Spooky or what?

How did it go?

Q   How do I tell between a sign and just something normal?

A   *Judge by what happens next. Once you start paying attention to what follows a particular unusual occurrence then you'll start to get a feel for what's pointing out something and what's not. Don't get obsessed by it though as usually signs are weird enough for us to pay attention rather than just everyday occurrences that we attribute meaning to.*

Q   I'm scared that I'll see portents of death or misery – how do I calm my fears?

A   *Hey, this is meant to be fun, not scary superstition! You're doing this in the spirit of joy, to be amazed at the strange patterns in the universe. You have to remember that and if you can't and you remain fearful then please stop looking for signs and just live your life. Happiness is the only goal.*

Q   My friends are scared of my uncanny ability to read signs – how do I avoid losing them?

A   *Ah, the witch-burning mob! I bet they come to you for advice when things are going badly for them though, right? Whenever we're worried we feel like we need a bit of reassurance. If you're a good friend, you can offer that reassurance without needing to read signs. Don't let it escalate to beyond a parlour game as then people start to get very frightened about what you may say next. Don't lose friends over something that's just a bit of harmless fun.*

35

Sensual scents

Smell can take you back to a particular time and place or it can lift your mood. Bring scentsual healing into your life.

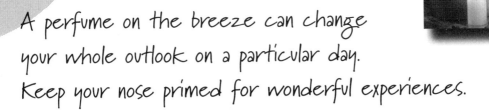

A perfume on the breeze can change your whole outlook on a particular day. Keep your nose primed for wonderful experiences.

I have a problem. I can't walk past lavender without picking a sprig and crushing it between my palms to inhale the fresh, floral scent. I am virtually incapable of just walking past a lavender patch. I have even leant into other people's gardens to get a sprig, which I do believe is stealing and therefore illegal. I am a criminal. The fact is that I have discovered the joy of aromatherapy. By aromatherapy, I don't mean a massage with smelly oils while tinkly music plays in the background. I mean that aromas are therapy to me. People have known the healing properties of different scents for centuries. They have a physiological effect on our brains that can change our moods.

Scent is used in so many different ways. Men and women wear scent to attract lovers, we use it to fragrance our homes and we even respond to it when it arouses our appetite for meals. Estate agents often recommend that clients wanting to

Here's an idea for you...

Make mulled wine off-season. While mulled wine is brilliant in winter months, you can also make it throughout the year for a warming drink that will scent your home beautifully. Stick a bunch of cloves in an orange and warm with two pints of water, a bottle of full-bodied red wine, a couple of oranges, some hot spices and 6 teaspoons of sugar (more or less according to personal taste) in a pan. You can also add a splash of brandy if you fancy it. Don't let it boil or the alcohol will evaporate.

sell their homes have something in the oven when people come to be shown around the house as the smell of baking immediately makes us feel as if we've entered somewhere warm and nurturing.

Some shops pump out scents into the street so that passers-by will be attracted into their shops. The whole science of scent is so complicated with base, middle and top 'notes' that you have specialists called 'noses' who work to create different scents for perfume houses. It's not as easy as 'this smells good' and 'this smells bad'. You may love the first 'top' note of a scent, apply it and then find an hour later you hate the way it has developed on your skin. If shopping for perfume, you should apply one on each wrist and then check again an hour later to see which you prefer. Never spray more than two in a day as you'll get very confused.

Your own personal body chemistry will also affect whether a scent suits you or not. Something that smells cloying on you may smell divine on your teenage sister who has different body chemistry. It is also why over time we sometimes change our tastes in perfume. When your body changes so does your natural scent, affecting the way that perfume smells on you.

Perfume is probably the most common way in which we respond to scent but essential oils are also a simple way to use the power of aromatherapy. You can use them in a variety of ways. You can mix a couple of drops of essential oil into a base oil like almond and get a helpful loved one to massage you with it. Or if helpful loved ones are in short supply, put a couple of drops into some hot water, cover with a towel, pop your head under it and inhale deeply. Most simple of all, put a couple of drops in your bath and languish in the aromatic, warm steam for as long as you can. Be careful when getting out, though, as oils will make your bath slippery.

'Smell is a potent wizard that transports you across thousands of miles and all the years you have lived.'
HELEN KELLER, author and activist

Defining idea...

Below is a short list of the sort of problems you may be facing and which essential oils can help remedy the situation.

- Anxiety: bergamot, lavender
- Bereavement: frankincense, rose
- Boredom: basil, peppermint
- Panic attacks: Neroli, Ylang Ylang
- Irritation: chamomile, lavender
- Sadness: bergamot, neroli
- Stress: lavender, sandalwood
- Nightmares: rock rose

You should also try and replace the harsh chemically-based scents of products in your home with the natural aromas of fruits, herbs and spices. This is better for your health and they smell just as pleasant and alluring.

Q   My husband has asthma and certain smells set him off. How do I experiment with smell without upsetting his health?

A   *In the bathroom, with the door closed. Smells in the bath are useful in that you can wash them away after you've had a bath. And you being lightly fragranced from your bath shouldn't set him off as you bathe with shampoos and soaps that are perfumed anyway and I'm assuming he finds those OK.*

Q   My boyfriend has bought a new cologne that is the same as the one my ex-boyfriend wore. How can I tell him to not wear it any more?

A   *Tell him the truth and say that you associate that cologne with a time that is over and not the pleasant time you are having with him now. Scent links in so closely with our emotions that it can be hard to disassociate negative memories from certain scents, just as much as it is difficult to forget a lovely memory tied in to some other particular perfume.*

Q   I can't afford expensive essential oils. Any suggestions?

A   *Use what's in your pantry. Clementines and oranges are a cheap way to get a citrus buzz. Either inhale deeply when eating them or fill a muslin bag with orange peel and hang it under the hot water tap in your bath. Cinnamon and cardamom are also glorious scents you can find quite cheaply in the supermarket. Let your nose lead you to cheaper alternatives to expensive oils and perfumes.*

36

A change is as good as a rest

Introduce change into your life to reignite your excitement and refresh your soul.

When you're stuck in a rut, start misbehaving until you find you manage to get yourself chucked out of it.

Every time you do something you build a neural pathway. The more times you repeat a particular behaviour, the stronger that pathway becomes. Eventually you'll do it almost on auto-pilot. This is great for saving time when doing things like driving or typing as who would want to learn those skills over and over again each time we needed them. The problem arises when things that shouldn't feel automatic become so. A good example is that of addictions. If your response to stress is to reach for the bottle or a cigarette, apart from the addictive qualities of the substance in question, you're conditioning yourself to drink or smoke to alleviate stress. If every time you felt stressed, you reached for your yoga mat instead, you'd build up a conditioning process that would link yoga with what to do if you get

Here's an idea for you...

If you use an electric toothbrush, buy a manual one. If you have a manual one, buy an electric one. Then alternate the two for a week. It will feel really weird to begin with and, while dentists the length and breadth of the country will be declaring a fatwa on me, you'll become more aware of what the inside of your mouth feels like. You'll probably decide to stick to the electric toothbrush though as they're the most fun you can have on your own in the bathroom. Ahem.

stressed. It would certainly be a huge benefit to your body and mind for you to build those associations.

Today, make a list of areas in your life where you'd like some changes to occur. Would you like to lose some weight? Be healthier? Spend less money? Get more time for hobbies? Make a big list and put everything you'd like to change in your life on there. Then pick just one thing that is bothering you. Forget the rest and put the list away until you have tackled that one thing. Having chosen one thing to deal with, make a new list of 10 things that you can do to tackle this problem. Suppose mine is to lose weight (actually that is one of mine – wow, this book is like a reality show!). My 10 things could be:

1   Drink 2 litres of water a day
2   Give up fizzy drinks
3   Eat at least five portions of fruit and vegetables a day
4   Join a weight-loss programme
5   Get half an hour of exercise three times a week

6   Walk an hour a day
7   Join a dance class
8   Go swimming
9   Not have seconds at meals
10 Switch to skimmed milk in tea

'Change in all things is sweet.'
ARISTOTLE, Greek philosopher

Defining
idea...

Then pick just one of those things. You don't have to go from 1 to 10; you can pick number six at random if you like. However, you must promise yourself that you will do this one thing faithfully for two weeks. Having done a fortnight of this, add another thing from your list for the next fortnight. Build it up until you're doing all 10 things. The two weeks of faithfully doing your lifestyle change is important because that is how long it takes us to form a habit. That was how long it took me to give up sugar in my hot drinks and now I can't bear to have even a few grains accidentally fall in my cup.

Pretty soon your changes will become habits. Once that happens, you should return to your list of things you'd like to change and see if there's something else you can tackle. Don't expect huge amounts of support from those around you as you are changing the familiar and that can be very disturbing for people who are afraid of change. If a person sees you as their 'ditzy' friend and suddenly you get very organised, they have to change their relationship to you from someone who takes care of you to someone who is on an equal footing and that can sometimes make them feel redundant. However, don't let the reservations of others stop you making enjoyable changes.

How did it go?

Q   I like my life – why should I have to change it?

A   *Change for change's sake is hardly ever fun or interesting. But you are reading about inner peace so I'm assuming you want something in your life to change. If you keep doing the same things over and over, you'll get the same result. It's fine to stick with the things you like in life but make a few little changes and see what benefits will accrue.*

Q   My wife says I'm having a mid-life crisis in making all these changes – am I?

A   *Yes, you are. We see a mid-life crisis as a bad thing but really a mid-life crisis is when we realise which goals we haven't achieved in life and always wanted to and we strike out to try to achieve those. The reason there is so much controversy around it is that for some men this sometimes means leaving their marriage and getting a much younger lover and a sports car. However, men are not stereotypes so don't let society tell you what your mid-life crisis should consist of. Do it your way, whatever that may be.*

Q   I want to make changes but my family aren't supportive. How do I convince them?

A   *While family support is a very useful thing, you don't necessarily need it to make changes in your own life. Start small so that nobody freaks out too much – maybe a different, bolder shade of lipstick. Then see where that leads you. Don't be disheartened by discouragement from others, your commitment is what really matters.*

37
Make and do

Unleash your creative side. Empty loo rolls optional.

You don't need a Blue Peter badge to bring creativity into your home and life.

The first time I visited my friend's house, I had a real urge to tidy it all up. There were paintings on the glass of his windows that his daughters had done, canvases and mobiles they had created, frames on the wall and doodles on furniture. As far as I was concerned, it was way too busy and stressful. However, over time, I realised that my friend had it right. Creativity in the home nurtures the physical building and it makes your home unique.

You don't have to be a creative wizard to make some nice things for your home. Get some nice thick paper from an art shop and some decorative stamps. Spend an evening chilling out at home, making stamped paper to line your drawers with. It is now considered quite old-fashioned to line your drawers but it is practical and pretty. You can even put a hand-embroidered handkerchief scented with lavender oil into your sock drawer to release a lovely scent each time you open it.

When I was little, my mother taught us how to do macramé as making pot-holders was terribly fashionable amongst her acquaintances. Since it is no longer the 70s, you may want to give the pot-holders a rest but you can still learn a textile craft like knitting or crocheting and make some very useful clothes for you and yours. In

Here's an idea for you...

Make your own cards or, if that's too girly for you, make your own CD covers. This can also be a great prank to play on your beloved, especially if you hate each other's taste in music. A mock CD cover with a quote from NME saying 'This is the worst sort of adult-orientated rock I've ever heard. My ears bled.' slipped quietly inside his favourite CD sleeve is sure to start a CD cover war, thereby whetting your creative appetite.

fact, in recent years knitting has been seen as trendy with many a celebrity turning to his or her needles to get rid of stress. Look for your local stitch n' bitch group, a fun place to swap ideas about what to make and to have a gossip with some new friends. It certainly beats being stuck indoors in front of the telly all the time. They even have cinema outings where you watch a film while silently getting on with your knitting (although I imagine that's for advanced people who can multi-task).

The next time something like a vase or a pot needs replacing, consider buying a cheap, plain one and decorating it yourself with some acrylic paints. Feel free to nick ideas from designers and make your own knock-offs of their expensive designs. You'll feel like you've accomplished something and the money you'll have saved will also be a delight.

I occasionally run workshops on spiritual art and the most common refrain I get from participants is 'I'm not artistic'. It is as if we've all been told that either you're good or you're bad at art and, if you're bad, you should never, ever presume to pick up a paintbrush. I say, poppycock (well, actually I say something ruder but it's always best to return to 1940s slang when wanting to say something obscene), anyone can create and everyone should create. The problem usually seems to be that we're scared someone will laugh at our efforts or crush our fledgling attempts at making something pretty. If you're scared of this, start small and perhaps string some beads together to make a new and distinctive bathroom light pull. This won't need to be critiqued by any budding art critics in your home and you can take it from there.

'All children are artists. The problem is how to remain an artist once he grows up.'
PABLO PICASSO

Defining idea...

The second you lose your inhibitions about creating things, you'll find a wealth of interesting ideas on what you can make yourself from tiaras for bridesmaids to mosaics for your bathroom. There's a world of creativity out there so get stuck in.

How did it go?

Q **Everything I make looks terrible – how do I gain better artistic skills?**

A *Get crafty and start making things again. If you don't know where to start, pick up a copy of Crafting Creativity. This is packed with ideas for making all manner of interesting things. You don't have to be fabulous with fiddly things; all it takes is enthusiasm and a willingness to practice. Remember those craft projects at school? Didn't you have fun making them? Well, do it again, and then freak out your mum by sending her your handiwork. She'll think she's stepped back in time.*

Q **My husband has told me to chuck out my creations as they're messing up the house – how do I get him to be nicer about it?**

A *Throw a strop. Well, OK, that's not productive. Ask him to name a room in the house that you can keep your creations in. Then limit your work to that area of the house. You could try selling it so that he starts to see the value in money of your work. It will also do your confidence a world of good.*

Q **My children insist upon painting and making me things and it is really great but the house is in danger of disappearing under their stuff. How do I avoid sentimentality?**

A *My niece is forever giving me drawings and then she watches eagle-eyed to see if I put it anywhere. I usually ask her to choose with me which one we like best to put on the fridge and the others have to go to either an art folder of her work or, if that's full, to the recycling bin. I explain that they recycle it into paper so that other little girls can draw on them too and that makes her feel happier about chucking some stuff away.*

38

Soul food

Cooking for those who hate it and those who love it.

You don't have to be a top chef to enjoy creating some happy memories in the kitchen.

Cooking is a science and an art. Some people excel in the science part and make very competent dishes through rigorously following a recipe, but those who truly love cooking turn it into an art by using judgement and skill to invent brand new dishes bursting with flavour.

I should come clean now and say that I am a terrible cook. This is despite having written about food and drink for well over a decade. I understand what makes a dish wonderful but I couldn't reproduce it for you in a month of Sundays. I also get worse at cooking the more nervous I get. If I'm hosting a party, I get very nervous indeed. So, to meet my aim of not poisoning the guests, I tend to stick to ordering in items from a deli that don't need anything more than heating up. It's kinder to both my guests and to my nerves.

Here's an idea for you...

I once invented a dinner party game called 'death row meals'. You decide what you'd have as your very last meal before execution. A less gruesome way to put it is what would be your 'desert island' meal. Think about this and cook/buy in for it/dine out on it this week.

You should always remember that the most important thing when cooking for others or yourself is that you enjoy the meal. Sometimes a dish will go disastrously wrong but cheese, biscuits, a drink and a laugh will save the evening. I once made the vegetarian daughters of a man I was madly in love with a nut roast. It came out with the consistency of a pâté so I pretended it was one, served it with crusty bread (which will hide a multitude of sins) and we all had an enjoyable meal.

The history of food is a fascinating subject and the term 'soul food' is one that describes the food of African Americans, particularly in the Southern States. One of the aspects of the brutality of slavery was that only off-cuts of meat and the throwaway parts of vegetables were given to the slaves to cook their own meals with. Being inventive and free of spirit, if not actually liberated yet, they cooked up new dishes that were partly based on some of the dishes of Africa. This shows that even if you oppress a people, they will find ways to keep themselves free at heart.

Soul food today, in the sense of this idea, is food that is made with heart and reminds you of a happy time in your life or comforts you when you are miserable. Whenever I get the blues, I ask my ma to make chicken livers as that's a soul food dish for me. What's yours? For many it is soup or a casserole. For others it could be a pudding or sausages and mash. Whatever the dish that pushes your buttons, eat it as often as you need to in order to stay happy and healthy.

If you're a bad cook like me, you can actually learn to be better. I now have a repertoire of seven dishes that I can cook very well because I've repeated them often enough. Practice does make perfect. Try and perfect even one dish and then soon you'll get bored of eating it and will have to learn another one. Through this process, bit by bit, you'll build up a library of dishes you can make from scratch that will impress anyone you cook for.

'Worries go down better with soup.'

Jewish Proverb

Defining idea...

If you love cooking and are pretty proficient at it, play 'pin the globe' dinners. Lay out a world map in front of you (or a globe if you have one), close your eyes and get someone to spin the map under you. Then put your finger down somewhere on the map. See where you've landed and find out on the internet what the principal dishes of that country or region are. Then try to cook them for dinner. This will ensure you don't get bored of making the same meals and you'll expand your knowledge of what people eat in other parts of the world.

How did it go?

Q **I made a meal and it turned out terribly – how do I get the confidence to step back in the kitchen?**

A   *OK, you need to get some crusty bread, some goats' cheese, a bit of olive oil, some basil leaves and a few cherry tomatoes. Toast the bread lightly under the grill, then pop it on a baking tray, drizzle some oil over it, put a generous chunk of goats' cheese on each toast and pop into a medium hot oven for about 10 minutes. Season and then garnish with the basil and tomatoes. Serve this simple snack to your family, who will love it, and then use their compliments to get you your confidence back to try some other things.*

Q **How can I convince my grandmother to give me her recipe for soup so that we can preserve it for future generations?**

A   *The short answer is you can't. I'm assuming you've already tried all the arguments about how it is a family heirloom and she should pass it on? The fact is that some members of the family are remembered for one superb dish and you remember the meal as they cooked it rather than as a recipe that can be duplicated. The piquant feeling is partly from the fact that the recipe went with them to the grave and you'll never have them or the dish again. Get her to make it for you as much as possible while she's still with you and show her your appreciation.*

39

Boredom-busting box

When you have fatigue of the spirit, discover this practical remedy for beating ennui.

I'm bored! I'm bored! I'm booooored! It's not just children who suffer from being bored to tears with everything — learn to deal with it without whining.

We've all had that experience when children meet every suggestion we make as to what they could do with 'That's boring!' and we know how frustrating that can be. However, when it happens to you as an adult, it is even worse.

One of the quickest ways to combat that feeling, though, is to think like a child. Build yourself a tent house in the garden by putting a throwover over the washing line and camping out inside your 'tent' house. You can read in there and drink daiquiris in the sunlit afternoon. When your partner returns home, convince him or her to come in with you and have a drink. It can be a silly way to 'shock' your sensible adult head out of boredom.

Here's an idea for you...

Go take a nap. No, really. When you're really bored and nothing is snapping you out of it, you can draw inspiration from your dreams and the best way to get a quick dream fix is to have a nap. The other benefit is that when you awake, you'll need to go freshen up, make a cup of tea and shake yourself out of sleep mode. This 'tricks' the brain into thinking that this second 'morning' is a new beginning and your boredom levels should plummet.

Along the same lines, dress up flamboyantly for the evening. Bring out the big pearls and diamonds and evening wear. Wear long gloves and feather boas. Definitely wear a tiara if you have one. Again you may startle your loved one when he comes home as he may think he's forgotten an anniversary. Just act normal and see how long it takes for him to crack and ask you what the hell is going on.

Another way to deal with the unexpected onslaught of boredom is to create a boredom-busting box. This should include the things that you think are fun but that you never get time to do. It could have a jewellery-making kit, a jigsaw, a chess set with a 'learn to play chess' book, some paints and small canvases, a manicure set and perhaps a tarot card set? Basically include anything that piques your interest but that you never get an opportunity to do and then have a rummage the next time boredom comes a-knocking.

Sometimes we get stung by boredom when we least require it; in the midst of a busy assignment for work or when we're organising an important function. We have a million and one things to do but no motivation to do anything. When that happens, step away from the computer and give yourself a half-hour break to go for a walk or listen to a radio show. Once that's done, return to your work and work for just one hour. You can have another break at the end of that hour. Incentivise yourself with things that you enjoy in order to get the work done. I usually say to myself that if I complete a certain section of work, I get to watch one murder mystery (my personal drug of choice).

'There's not a joy the world can give like that it takes away,
When the glow of early thought declines in feeling's dull decay.'
A rather jaded LORD BYRON

Defining idea...

Movies generally are a great way to shift boredom as there are so many. Join your local library as they often have DVDs and videos for a much cheaper rental than video stores. You can also start a DVD library with your friends and swap movies that you've each enjoyed. You know which genres you like so circulate each person's preferences about and enjoy a free movie exchange. Also investigate old films that you can pick up very cheaply in charity shops and stalls; there's a treasure trove of comedies and dramas that not only tell a fantastic story but also show some beautiful costumes and hairstyles from the 40s and 50s. Part of the appeal of films like *Breakfast at Tiffany's* is Audrey Hepburn's fabulous clothes. Guaranteed to stop plaintive cries of 'I'm bored!'.

How did it go?

Q   I'm still bored – help?!

A   *Och, you'll just have to sit with it then. Sometimes there's no shaking boredom and when that happens, you should just let it happen. Sigh loudly if it helps, go annoy someone by leaning over their shoulder and seeing what they're doing, go make yourself useful and start dinner. Or just veg out listlessly in front of TV. Rest assured it won't last forever.*

Q   My children are always saying they're bored – what should I do to entertain them?

A   *Exercise normally tires out young minds. How about taking them swimming or going for a walk? Walks are especially good as they're free and you get to see different things at different times of the year. Go and collect conkers in autumn and make daisy chains in summer. They're bound to cease whining about being bored if they're in the open air.*

Q   I feel really apathetic about everything – is this the same as boredom?

A   *No, it's a close relation but a bit more dangerous. You can snap out of boredom much easier than you can out of apathy. Once you get that particular malaise it can be hard even to motivate yourself to do the things that will shift your problem. Talk to somebody about it. If there is a clear reason why you're feeling this way then it may pass once the situation is over but, if nothing seems wrong and you still feel this way, consider talking to your doctor about it as you shouldn't suffer in silence.*

40

Become an anorak

Why passion is your biggest ally in finding inner peace.

Reignite your love for a particular hobby, sport or thing and you'll find that all aspects of your life improve.

Do you feel jaded about the world and your place in it? You need to get some of your passion back. One of the best ways to retain passion is to have something you care deeply about. For some people this is a particular sport that they study obsessively, either as a participant or as an observer. For others it can be something like opera or art or even the classic anorak activity – trainspotting. Being a geek is now very chic as it shows that you are still excited about something while all around you people are turning apathetic.

Think back to the last time you spoke about something and your eyes were glistening and you were talking nineteen to the dozen. If you can't remember, ask your partner or your friends to let you know what you talk about most excitedly. When you find your passion, you can read about it till the cows come home and still not get bored.

Here's an idea for you...

Join a club or go to an introductory club meet. This can be for anything at all. You'll find in clubs of like-minded people that there are some who know more than you and some who don't; this unevenness in knowledge makes things constantly interesting as you're bound to learn something new or impart some knowledge. And you can't pay for the invigorating enthusiasm of some folks out there. Get inspired!

Passions are also a way of entering 'the zone'. The zone is a state of being within which you lose all sense of time and space because you are so lost in what you're doing. The more time you can spend in this pleasurable state, the better it is for your health and happiness. Your blood pressure is lower – unless of course bungee-jumping is your passion of choice – and your stress levels end up being very low.

One of my passions is Agatha Christie's *Poirot* novels. I like the era she wrote in, I like the TV film dramatisations (though I prefer David Suchet as the Belgian detective rather than Peter Ustinov) and I love the bloodcurdling murders. I can watch them on a loop and I can bore anyone with any aspect of Poirot lore.

My other passion is the BBC adaptation of *Pride and Prejudice*. I have seen it hundreds of times and can recite the lines back to you. It is a fairly useless passion as they're not much I can do with it beyond watch it over and over again (and there's only so much pause and play you can do over Colin Firth in a bath). It is also a bit sad and a bit embarrassing and my sister will scream if I watch it in front of her again but it makes me happy whenever I watch it in one sitting. A good way to find your passion is to pay attention when your family groans when you mention something. That is an easy way to know that this is something you love enough to bang on about it all the time.

Some people take their passions and turn them into careers. While this is not suitable in all passions, it is certainly a way to make a living out of something you'd be willing to do for free. If you love making models, perhaps you can sell them to people who don't enjoy making them but like owning them? If you have a passion for baking, perhaps you can supply your cakes to a local café?

'*Only passions, great passions, can elevate the soul to great things.*'

DENIS DIDEROT, author and philosopher

Defining idea...

Even if you can't find a way to make money from your passion, you should give a reasonable amount of time to it. Not to the exclusion of everything else but a regular unit of time in which you can enjoy your hobby. Make this time special to you and let your family know that they shouldn't disturb you when you're indulging your hobby but also make time for them so they don't start resenting your passion.

How did it go?

Q **I don't think I've ever felt passionate about something – how do I find my inner anorak?**

A *Most people can remember something they loved doing as a child, be it collecting cards or watching Star Trek or something, but some of us don't remember ever feeling obsessive about anything. In such a case you have to undertake an investigation into what your passions are. Try and do something completely new each month, like a painting class or rock climbing. Gauge how much you enjoy each activity and start to do those you really enjoy regularly. You'll learn more and more as you progress in your chosen hobby or sport. You only gain anorak status after a sustained time doing something you love. Good luck!*

Q **My husband is a football nerd and I find it excruciatingly boring. How do I stop him boring me with information about football?**

A *In the parallel universe where I am Supreme Ruler, football has been banned and anyone who even thinks to mention it is tickled to death. However, since you don't live in my universe, you have to find another way to deal with it. Get a hobby of your own and ask your husband to only discuss football with his mates rather than you. If he ignores your request, start telling him in minute detail about your new hobby. He'll definitely stop very quickly.*

41

Grieving well

When your inner world is shattered by the departure of a loved one, learn how to rebuild your life one piece at a time.

When someone you love dies, you don't have to die with them. Don't allow your grief to stop your internal clock.

The first time someone I loved died unexpectedly, I was completely shocked that the world didn't stop. I couldn't understand how things were meant to continue normally, why the whole edifice of human life didn't just crash down around our ears. I kept saying to my friends 'What will happen now?' as I genuinely couldn't believe that everything would return to a sense of normality. However, it did. It was a different normality as it was a world without my friend Gareth in it but it was normality nonetheless.

Then, just as I realised that it was possible to get over an untimely death, another very young friend of mine – Neil – died unexpectedly too. This time round I was much better prepared. I knew that the grave into which we threw fresh herbs was not where Neil resided, his spirit was somewhere else. I cried long and hard but then I stopped crying. In the Indian subcontinent, it is believed that crying for too long can cause the soul of the person who has died to become tied to the living rather than moving on to the great beyond.

Here's an idea for you...

Call your friends and take 'if there's anything I can do' seriously. People are often crippled with doubt as to whether they should contact you if you're suffered the loss of a loved one – especially if it was unexpected and they died young or tragically – so give them the easy way out. You call them. You ask for what you need. And if you need nothing but to drop out of society for a while then let them know that too so that embarrassment and fear of upsetting you doesn't make them lose touch with you.

Death and dying are one of the last great social taboos. We don't know what to say to someone who has suffered a loss and we don't know what to do if we're the one who has suffered a loss. In other cultures there are specific rituals connected with death and dying. The widow spends a certain amount of time in which she cannot leave the home, ensuring that someone has to come and visit her or none of her shopping gets done. This provides for company. There are also rules about not lighting a fire in the house where a death has taken place; this encourages people in the community to bring food to your house. Again, this gives company at a time when we feel shattered, lost and confused.

Community is very important at this time and as we become more and more detached as a society our sense of community is dying. This makes looking after the bereaved a difficult thing to do. People may not even know that you've suffered a loss, given how rarely we manage to talk to each other. A friend of mine only discovered that Neil, who I worked with and saw daily, had died when he called out of the blue to ask me some advice about journalism. His response was amazing; as a psychologist he was trained in counselling and he insisted on giving me a session about bereavement. It was a practical help at a time that I was in pieces.

Massage may be the last thing on your mind if you've just lost someone but once the initial couple of months are over and you are beginning to get your bearings, book yourself in for a Hawaiian massage. This is called Lomi Lomi and is very effective in dealing with grief as the practitioner is not just massaging your body, he or she is channelling healing love into you and you do feel the effects of having that done to you. It is a compassionate massage, as far removed from just a physical pampering as you can get. Book it in almost as medicine and I wish you future happiness and a heart well-healed.

'Give sorrow words; the grief that does not speak whispers the o'er-fraught heart and bids it break.'

Defining idea...

WILLIAM SHAKESPEARE

181

How did it go?

Q **Will I be betraying the memory of my boyfriend if I start dating again?**

A *No, you won't. If your boyfriend loved you then he'll want you to be happy and you can't be happy if you're stuck in the past, grieving forever. Once you feel ready, start slowly dating again but be prepared for more tears and be gentle with yourself. You will get over this.*

Q **My brother inherited the business that my father and I built up because my dad hadn't updated his will. How can I grieve properly when I'm still so angry with my father?**

A *It is not uncommon to feel anger toward the departed; you feel left behind or in the lurch – this is especially so in your case. Is it possible for you to speak to your brother for a more equitable resolution? If not, think carefully whether contesting the will can come to any good. It may be better for you to consider the experience and skills your father gave you in business as his legacy to you. Start your own business and start letting go of your anger toward him.*

Q **I can't imagine getting over the death of my wife – it's been a year and time hasn't healed. Is that cliché true?**

A *Time does heal. It doesn't make you forget. It won't stop you missing your wife but it will make it easier to start living again. You will end up laughing and living fully again – you owe it to yourself, your family and, most of all, to your wife. Take it slow and don't lose heart.*

42

Colour me happy

The colours you surround yourself with have an impact on your mood. Find out which you can use and how.

Leading a 'colourful' life isn't just about seducing your gardener; it's about harnessing the power of different colour energies.

Colour is basically light of different wavelengths and frequencies that are filtered through our eyes to make things look the colour they do. We really only see the three primary colours – red, blue and green – and our brains mix up variations of these three to create the other colours. There are seven colours in the spectrum and they all have different wavelengths and frequencies.

We can use the knowledge of how each of these colours affects us to use colour in healing and to affect us positively. Apart from the obvious trick of dressing in a particular colour, you can also take colour baths, gaze at colour screens and even change your lightbulbs to create colour rooms.

In the Indian Vedic system of healing, the human body has seven chakras (centres of energy), each of which corresponds to a particular colour:

- Crown – violet
- Third eye – indigo
- Throat – blue
- Heart – green
- Solar plexus – yellow
- Sacral – orange
- Base – red

Here's an idea for you...

Tie a blue ribbon around your phone handset or have a blue ribbon mobile charm. If you have an important business meeting or interview, wear a blue necktie or a blue necklace. Blue is the colour of the throat chakra, facilitating easy communication and the ability to persuade others. It doesn't matter if you believe it or not, even the thought of 'what if it works' will give you a little extra confidence.

Wearing the colour of a chakra that is blocked in you can have an amazing effect on your life. My solar plexus (located in your middle, just under your ribs) was blocked and cleared through wearing lots of yellow. You can discover the state of your own chakras through this exercise. Sit comfortably cross-legged with your hands in your lap and your bum bones solidly into the floor. Close your eyes and take three deep breaths, in and out through the nose. Then imagine a silvery white light entering from somewhere up in the ceiling into your crown chakra (the top of your head).

Imagine it going down into your third eye chakra (in the middle of your forehead) and then down to your throat chakra, then your heart, then your solar plexus, then your sacral (mid-way between your belly button and your genitals) and the base (the underside of your genitals). As you imagine this light going down through your chakras, feel for any blockages or the impression of shapes and colours. This should flow quite easily if you're not blocked anywhere but a blocked chakra will feel sluggish and may give you the impression of the colour brown or grey. You should then wear the corresponding colour to try and clear that particular chakra.

'The purest and most thoughtful minds are those which love colour the most.'
JOHN RUSKIN, art critic and author

Defining idea...

If you find all this talk of chakras a bit too weirdy-beardy then just know that colours have different effects on us. The impression 'red rag to a bull' is a good way of thinking of it. Studies have shown that if you paint school walls a bright red, the degree of disruption and discipline problems go up whereas a calming colour like pale blue works very well. Here are some colour associations with the main seven colours of the spectrum:

- Violet – spirituality, link to divinity
- Indigo – intuition, higher knowledge
- Blue – communication, calming
- Green – balance, harmony
- Yellow – intelligence, cheerfulness
- Orange – healing, creativity
- Red – courage, strength, high energy

You can use this information to work creatively with colours. Try and find some indigo-coloured pillow cases and see how this colour of intuition affects your dreams. Wear red when you're feeling fatigued and see if that gives you the requisite oomph. Have fun with it and see what discoveries you can make.

You can also use your knowledge in the way that you decorate your home. It may be good to have a calming colour like blue in the bedroom. They say that red stimulates the appetite so perhaps avoid it in the dining room if you're trying to stick to a diet. The colour green has also been associated with money so it is a good choice for a home office.

Q   Aren't I too old to wear bright colours?

A   Na-ah. How could you think that? You're never too old for colours. Colour doesn't have an age limit. I was also once told by someone that fat people shouldn't wear bright colours. I soon put them straight. While black may be slimming, bright colours make you look vibrant and alive so don't forsake them irrespective of your age or shape.

Q   How can just wearing a colour affect my mood?

A   You're responding to light and a frequency when you see colour so your perception is what is making the colour you see. As such you can change your perception with the colour you see. Rather than try and find some fancy scientific explanation for you, I would recommend that you experiment and find out which colours cheer you up the most and then start using them liberally.

Q   My boyfriend has painted our bathroom a sickly mint green. Any arguments against mint green?

A   I met a phenomenal healer once (who doesn't want to be named) who told me that green is terrible for cancer as it promotes growth and what you want is an orange to burn up and halt the cancerous growth. However, that is a very specific case and I'm afraid I don't have much against green for you otherwise. Jealousy? You could say the bathroom is making you more jealous of his friends but that's a bit of a long shot. Just be honest and ask him to change it.

How did
it go?

187

43

Switching off

From the internet to mobile phones, we are always switched on and plugged in. Turn it all off and see what happens.

The buzz of electricity is always with us. Try reverting to a slower, more calming time when bleeps and ringtones didn't interrupt your every thought.

I recently arrived from London at a house I was minding for a friend in Sussex to find all the lights out. He has an electricity meter and, while he'd been away, the electricity paid for on his card had run out. As it was 6pm, the shop where you could top up the card was shut. I'd have to spend the night with no TV and no lights. It was winter so it was already pitch black. I lit some candles and discovered that you can singe your eyebrows if you try to read by candlelight. I made a hot drink on the gas stove and then carried it up to bed. Lying in bed I started to feel bored as it was still only about 6.30. Luckily I had a battery-operated radio and I listened to that for an hour. Then I turned in to bed at 7.30pm, the earliest I'd ever gone to bed. The

Here's an idea for you... If it is at all possible, remove all electricals from your bedroom. Only have low lighting and see how it feels for a while. If you like it, keep it like that; if you don't, ask yourself why you need to be so switched on, even in your room of rest and recuperation?

next day I woke up well rested but I virtually ran to the shop to get the electricity back on.

The experience made me think of how things must have been before electricity, when people used the sunset to tell them when to go to bed. The winter must have been a cosy time of rest and relaxation while the summer would have been busy work all day long. I am a modern enough girl not to hanker back to those times but I do think that switching off some of our gadgets and gizmos is great for the search for inner peace. Try to do it for one day or even a few hours and see what it feels like.

Someone I know once referred to the mobile phone as an electronic leash. The office could call you to heel at any moment. You are always available. Some offices pride themselves on a good work–life balance but this often means blurring the boundaries between work and home life. I think your home life suffers if you're on the laptop or mobile phone when you're with your family. It is far better to be out of the home from 8–6 and completely present with your family when you're back than it is to be doing 'flexi-time' and always be checking mails and taking calls, even through meals.

If there's one thing you should never do it is to take a call during a meal without apologising profusely to the people you're dining with. I once left my boyfriend having a meal by himself in a restaurant because he had spent 40 minutes on the phone to work. I just walked out the restaurant and he didn't even notice. He said later that he thought I'd gone to the loo. I hadn't and he found out that I had left because the waiter told him. He was annoyed at how rude I'd been to do that. I was annoyed at how rude he'd been to invite me to dinner and then spend 40 minutes on the phone. Needless to say, we're exes now.

'He that can take rest is greater than he that can take cities.'
BENJAMIN FRANKLIN, One of the Founding Fathers of the USA

Defining idea...

Another bugbear is the internet. You can spend hours and hours trawling through site after site. Do you remember when we had books? In those funny old-fashioned places called libraries? I say head back there. Oftentimes the information you get on the internet is unregulated and inaccurate. My cousin was described as the daughter rather than stepdaughter of her horrid stepmother on Wikipedia. I was having none of it and changed it to a more accurate description, but it is one small example of how you should take everything you read on the internet with a pinch of salt. Better still, turn it off for a bit and do something quaint like read a book.

How did it go?

Q   My work doesn't allow me to switch off. How can I get that degree of peace?

A   *Even if you're a top surgeon, you will eventually be allowed a holiday so use that holiday to switch off. Consider going somewhere that your phone doesn't work. Or stay at home and warn everyone that you will be incommunicado and just unplug everything. It will feel like quite a dramatic change.*

Q   I found this idea too hard to grasp – do I have to switch off in order to achieve inner peace?

A   *Not necessarily. Buddhists believe that once you recognise the true nature of all things, the illusion will fall away and you will realise that you are separate from nothing, not even the annoying phones and beepers. Of course, it's harder to realise the true nature of anything when you're stuck in the middle of all that noise but we have it on good authority that it is possible.*

Q   My parents worry if my phone is switched off – how can I do that to them?

A   *Try just a couple of hours and pre-warn them that you're going to do it. After all, we all survived quite well without mobile phones in the past and they don't work when you're underground or in a low coverage area so just imagine that you're in a meeting at work and have had to switch it off. Your parents will completely understand that you can't be reached at all times of the day.*

44

Promises, promises

Making your word your bond will enhance not only your life but also your reputation.

Promising to do something is not just about the words but is all in the action that follows the promise.

We've all had to break promises in our lives. Sometimes something comes up that we can't avoid, or we get sick, or we make an excuse and hide. Breaking promises is not the worst crime of the century but it is one that will chip away at your sense of self. Every time you break a promise, you are saying to the universe and to yourself that you can't be trusted. It's not the other person you're letting down, it's yourself.

The easiest way to avoid breaking promises is to think long and hard before you make them. If you promise to scatter Uncle Albert's ashes in the Nile, he's not going to be too happy with the Thames estuary if you can't make it to Egypt in the year he dies. Only make a promise if you are certain you can keep it. If your circumstances change and you can't keep it, let the other person know as soon as possible and try to make amends (in the case of Uncle Albert send him with your sister on holiday so she can do the deed instead).

Here's an idea for you...

Promise a child you know that you will do something with them next weekend. Then keep that promise. It's a zero tolerance approach to promise-keeping as no-one can bear to see crestfallen little faces if you break a promise to a child. So you know that you'll definitely keep that one and that's a start. If you don't even manage to keep that promise then you're clearly not meant for promises and you should never make another one as long as you live. Bear in mind that marriage is also a promise so that means you can't ever get married either. Or hold down a job.

Always keep a copy of your promises. This may sound weird but how will you remember to keep your promise if you don't write it down? One of my best friends makes promises to come to things with me with every intention of coming but because he doesn't keep a diary, I have to call him the day before to remind him. It means that things sometimes get cancelled but he refuses to have a diary. He just taps his temple and says 'it's like a steel trap'. Clearly, Raj, it is not a steel trap, it's a sieve.

Sometimes people emotionally blackmail us into making promises. If that happens to you a lot, you have to get tougher. Or better still, play them at their own game and make them give you promises to do stuff. You tend to find that the people who are insistent that you not let them down are the ones who find it impossible to keep their promises to you. It is a form of selfishness that needs to be banished from your life.

The most important promises are those you make to yourself. You must always keep these. If you promise yourself that you'll have a glass of champagne when you achieve a certain goal, start saving for that champagne now as lack of money is no good excuse for breaking a promise to yourself. You should build up faith in yourself by making small promises to yourself each day. This is sometimes called a 'to do' list but to do lists often have things left undone on them. You need to just pick a couple of things that you promise yourself you'll get done each day and then just do them. Sometimes they can be easy things that you'd have done anyway but other days pick something that stretches you – that phone call you don't want to make or a scan at the doctor's you've been putting off. Day by day you will trust yourself more and more. It is wonderful when you yourself know, beyond a shadow of a doubt, that your word is your bond.

'Commitment is what transforms a promise into reality.'
ABRAHAM LINCOLN, 16th President of the USA

Defining idea...

197

How did it go?

Q I do try to keep my promises but what can I do if something else comes up?

A   *Does something always come up or is it a very rare occasion? If it is rare then of course make your apologies and re-organise to do whatever you promised another time or to make it up to the person on the receiving end of your promise. However, if this is a regular occurrence then think about your commitment to your promises. Don't make any for a while if you think you won't be able to keep them.*

Q My girlfriend always breaks her promises to me – should I leave her?

A   *Depends what the promises are. If it is to watch footie with you and she runs away at the last minute, well, she may just be preserving her own sanity. If it is a promise to stop drinking and she's an alcoholic, then you have a bigger problem. You need to have an open and honest discussion with her about how you feel when she lets you down time and time again. Give her a chance to make amends.*

Q Is there ever a graceful way to back out of a promise?

A   *Nope, it's almost always a bit of a messy way out. Having said that, thinking about how to save the situation for the person you promised something to is usually quite effective. Think whether there is someone who can replace you or if you can help in a way that will mend the effects of your broken promise.*

45

A rare treat

Take back your pleasure in treats by limiting them to rare occasions.

Treats every day become a normal part of your life. This can make you feel bored rather than excited at the thought of another one.

When I was little, we got a cardboard box and string to make a car for ourselves. None of this mini-BMW-for-kids lark. Now before I start on a rant about 'In my day...' it is true to say that children are used to more and more presents, toys and gadgets now than ever before. We didn't have such a vast array of things to nag our parents for when we were younger and also it was considered immoral then to 'spoil' your child. I feel sorry for today's parents as that moral high ground has been taken away. We are a consumer society with a big emphasis on getting the best for our children. This means that something that would have been considered a treat back in my youth is considered a weekend normality now. I can't remember ever getting presents when it wasn't my birthday or Christmas. Perhaps if an uncle came to visit or I went to a party where there was a party bag to take home with you.

Here's an idea for you...

When I was young my cousin and I would have 'chocolate day'. This was each Friday and we weren't allowed any chocolates on any other day but on Friday we got to have about 20 of them. This made us feel very, very happy (and a little sick) on Fridays. Pick a treat that you only have once a week and stick to it so that it really does feel special when you have it.

However, my niece and nephew get new toys almost every other weekend. They play with it for a couple of hours and then it lies forgotten in their rooms.

This feeling of immediate gratification and then disappointment is also prevalent in adults nowadays. A woman who works hard all week may go shopping on a Saturday and buy herself a lipstick or a top to feel better about the hard week just gone by. However, that happiness is short-lived and needs to be topped up again and again in order for any future treats to have any effect. Strangely the way we get that pleasurable experience is not from getting more and more treats but from getting fewer and fewer of them.

Anticipation is part of the joy of a real treat. It is a treat because it is rare and you look forward to it. Think of how lovely it is to have treats on holidays, forgetting the diets and saving and scrimping for a couple of weeks of unadulterated pleasure. Now imagine if you could blow out on restaurant meals and ice creams and all sorts of good things every day of the year. You'd soon feel the pinch in both your pocket and your too-tight-now trousers.

Re-introduce the idea of a rare treat into your life. If you love cream buns, have them just once a month and really relish the experience. If you really want to make it a treat, go and have a cream tea at a restaurant. The point is not to deny yourself but to save it for once in a while so that it feels like a special occasion. You value things that you save and wait for much more than those you can get in a heartbeat. Find yourself a 'treat buddy' who enjoys the same things as you and put a date in your diary each month to enjoy your particular treat. If it is something expensive and complicated like scuba diving then adjust how often you do it accordingly. However, don't go for any more frequent than once a month as then it's not really a treat.

'Rare indulgence produces greater pleasure.'
JUVENAL, Roman poet

Defining idea...

In between times if you're really feeling deprived, give your treat buddy a call and talk about what you'll do when you go for your treat. This will get you revved up but you won't actually be giving in to temptation. Keep each other on the straight and narrow. The great thing about this is that you can also teach delayed gratification to your children, which, as we all know, makes for much more pleasant human beings than snotty-nosed brats who want everything NOW.

201

How did it go?

Q   **How can I avoid the temptation to treat myself all the time?**

A   *Make a promise to yourself that you will gratify your need for a treat on a given day, say a week from now, and then make a note in your diary. When the day comes around, faithfully go and keep your promise to yourself. Each time you feel tempted, look in your diary to see how near treat day actually is.*

Q   **I work really hard, why should I be denying myself treats?**

A   *This is what economists call the 'entitlement' argument for spending. You feel entitled to have a treat but haven't you been compensated for working hard with money? You have the money in the bank from having worked hard, why do you need to 'prove' to yourself that you work hard by treating yourself? Aren't you aware of the hard work already? Also, spending your hard-earned cash on treats means that you have to work harder to keep achieving the treats you are giving yourself for working hard. It's a vicious circle whereas saving your money could help you cut back your hours and not work so hard.*

Q   **Why do I always feel guilty if I'm treating myself, even rarely?**

A   *You feel as though you're not worthy of a treat and that's very sad. You must cease to have this attitude at once. Really enjoy your treat because you have saved up for it and you've earned it so why shouldn't you enjoy it? Don't be your own party-pooper.*

46

Family time

Rediscover the pleasure in spending time with people you could potentially harvest organs from.

You can choose your friends but you can't choose your family so you may as well get on rather than fight. You're in it together.

Families can represent some of the best and most difficult relationships of our lives. They are key in the development of our personalities and our outlooks. The saying that the 'apple doesn't fall far from the tree' is a truism, although you do not have to follow the same patterns as your family if you don't want to. You can be the first from your family to go to university if that's your dream. Don't let the notion that 'no-one in our family does that' stop you from forging your own path.

It is limitations like these that often cause us to lose touch with our families. We assume that all family interaction will involve arguments and recriminations. However, it doesn't have to be like that. It may be that you first just need to spend some time with your family, maybe not even talking. Get some tickets to the cinema or rent a DVD to watch together. Just don't automatically snap if Aunt Maud keeps asking what's happening. Be patient and appreciate that you're watching the DVD together not to see what happens in the film but to spend some family time together.

Here's an idea for you...

Family dining is a fantastic idea as this is the time you can share properly with each other what your day's been like and also arguments over the dinner table are never as serious as those you have without a plate of food in front of you. Reinstate this family tradition so you see the faces of your loved ones at least one meal a day.

Regular time spent with your extended family will ensure that holidays like Christmas aren't pressure cooker affairs with everyone flying off the handle. Pick a useful activity that you can all do together and use it as a bonding exercise. Perhaps you and your siblings could come by a couple of weekends before Christmas and help your mum paint a ceiling or two. Sprucing up the family home will be an aid to your parents but will also give you a chance to chat while doing something instead of at the dinner table. Things rarely get emotionally charged if you have a paintbrush in your hand. You will also have achieved something fantastic together and can admire your handiwork when you relax with a cup of tea afterwards.

Most people have families that mean well and we often forget that in the sprint to be the one on the 'I am right' box. Lose a couple of arguments but win the fight to be a loving family. No matter how eccentric your family is, those are the things that you'll miss when they're gone and you're telling your grandchildren about what they were like. Don't forget birthdays and special anniversaries as it's remembering those days that gel a family together. Imagine your mother's surprise when she calls her sister to discover that you sent her a birthday card without her prompting you. She may very well need to take a seat and she may wonder if you're feeling quite well. Behaving in a loving and considerate way toward your family may well have them thinking you have a terminal illness and are making your peace before going but reassure them that it's just because you love them.

One of the best gifts we have been given by our parents is fascinating stories about what our grandparents and great-grandparents were like. It was much better than the plot of *Titanic* to hear about real romantic missing beaus and great-aunts who pined away for a love lost. This was our own history and Spielberg couldn't produce a better picture if he tried his best. Chatting around a fireplace was one of the first things that ancient families did. Now that fireplaces are in short supply, just sit and chat around the coffee table. You'll be surprised at what you discover about your own lineage.

'Families are like fudge – mostly sweet with a few nuts.'

Anon

Defining idea...

205

How did it go?

Q   My family is always having in-fights. How can we stop?

A   Call a family meeting and appoint the least argumentative person as chair. Make a commitment to try to see the other person's point of view before starting to argue. Of course it'll probably descend into quite a slanging match but at least there'll be some peace and quiet as most people will stop talking to each other. If you're really worried, consider talking to a family counselling centre.

Q   How do I convince my sister not to move abroad, as I'd miss her so much?

A   That's a tough one as your sister has her own life to lead. You don't want her to feel bad and guilty while she's abroad and also if you manage to convince her to stay, she may resent you for the missed opportunity. Let her go and visit her as often as you can afford. Think how you'd want her to act if you had a marvellous opportunity to live abroad. Give her the same chance.

Q   My mother is so critical of me that I avoid going home during the holidays – how can I get her to stop?

A   Visit more often. No, seriously, she probably goes into criticism overdrive because she sees you so rarely that she has to get it all in at once. If you visit more often, it'll be spread over the year and won't seem like such an assault at Easter or Christmas. Also, have a quiet word with her when no-one else is about and explain how you feel when she criticises you. She probably doesn't even realise she's doing it.

47

Who are you?

Imagine you've been invited to a fancy dress party. Which character most appeals to you? Find out what your fantasy person says about your inner being.

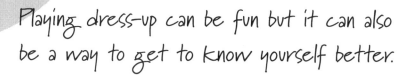

Playing dress-up can be fun but it can also be a way to get to know yourself better.

We play so many different roles in life. We're children, parents, siblings, employees, friends, spouses or lovers and several other roles. This can sometimes cause a difficulty in figuring out who you are once all those roles are stripped away. Are you seductive or are you shy? Are you brave or nervous? Cruel or kind? Lively or dull? There are so many different personality possibilities and usually we are different things at different times.

Have you ever been to a fancy dress party? There are two types of people in the world; those who love fancy dress parties and those who simply won't come if you tell them it's fancy dress. I am firmly in the first camp but I have known a lot of people in the second camp. I have noticed that people in the first camp are extrovert and mouthy while those in the second one don't like to draw attention to themselves. It's not that they're shy, necessarily; more that they don't want to stand out in a crowd.

Here's an idea for you...

Have a fancy dress party and invite everyone to dress as the historical or fictional character they most identify themselves with. It'll be a real eye-opener as to what you and your friends are like... just be a bit nervous if everyone turns up dressed as Cybermen.

I pay attention to whom I choose to dress up as at fancy dress parties. My friend had a Rocky Horror party and I was Magenta. He had a 'Biblical characters' party and I was Salome. At an '80s TV shows' party I was Diana, the villain from the alien invasion show V. At that party I was surrounded by Wonderwomen. It looked like a Wonderwoman convention. I have, over the years, realised that my inner personality, the one I wish I could show a bit more of, is that of the vamp, the bad girl. This is because I've always been a good girl so my 'dress-up' persona is all about where I lack balance. I'm just not bad enough.

My very outgoing friend always wears something bizarre and elaborate like an ape costume or a storm-trooper's outfit. The thing about this, though, is that the suit wears him. He doesn't have to do anything as the outfit is wacky and impressive enough to carry him through the evening with no effort at all on his part. Plus his face is covered so no-one can really tell what he's thinking. It is a shy person's dress-up outfit really. So this wild and wacky friend of mine is actually a little boy wanting to hide from the world behind a big gorilla costume. Now before the psychologists in the audience start hurling things at me, I should say that this is not a scientific method. It's just a bit of fun that I've noticed over the years. You can sort of tell who will go for which costume because our personalities determine what we are attracted to. Most interestingly, the costume we choose can indicate how we want others to see us. I'd like folks to think of me as danger-ous and sexy (when really I'm a fluffy bunny who wouldn't hurt a fly). See what your cos-tume says about you. Here's my unscientific idea about what different costumes say:

- Superman: hero complex, usually exhib-ited by nerds
- Cleopatra: seductive tart
- Wonderwoman: tart with nice legs and dominatrix tendencies
- Gladiator: exhibitionist, possibly with a very close relationship with your mum
- Godzilla: More money than sense – do you know how much it costs to hire one of those?!
- Pharaoh: control freak who hogs all the dips
- Dolphin: control freak who forces people to laugh at his lame jokes
- Devil: wannabe bad boy or girl but really rather sweet and unassuming
- Mobster: someone who doesn't like fancy dress and wanted to get away with wearing a suit and a hat that could be removed when necessary
- Fairy: annoying person who thinks they're being pixie-like but really are just being passive-aggressive

Defining idea…

Jeeves: *Shall I lay out one of your novelty handkerchiefs for you today, Sir?*
Bertie: *Oh, come off it, Jeeves! Everyone wears things with initials on them nowadays.*
Jeeves: *I thought the practice was restricted to those who were in danger of forgetting their names, Sir.*
P.G. WODEHOUSE, adapted from *The Code of the Woosters*

How did it go? **Q   I hate fancy dress parties and doubt I'd dress up as anyone – how do I get the insights without the silly costume?**

A   *Think back to a movie you may have seen that particularly moved you. Which character did you identify with most? The hero who always got the girl and saved the world? Or his geeky genius best friend or the baddie who wanted to blow up the world? Try and step into those lives and see if there's a personality that sits particularly well with you.*

Q   My boyfriend likes me to dress up as Snow White – should I be worried?

A   *Depends on whether he asks the dwarves to come along too. No, don't be worried. Do it if you find it fun and don't if you don't want to. Human sexuality is bizarre at times and dress-up and playacting is just one element of it. Enjoy yourself whatever or whoever you are.*

Q   I love dressing up as Louise Brooks, the silent film actress. Is it weird to go for that look daily?

A   *Not at all! The Louise Brooks bob is often in fashion and the clothes of that era were very flattering. I'd be more worried if you liked say Superman's sartorial sense as wandering around with your pants on the outside is never a good idea. Or a good look.*

48

Lottery life

If money were no object, where would you live? How would you live? How and with whom would you spend your days? Use this information to produce a plan for happiness.

Winning the lottery may seem like a pipe dream but leading the life you'd have if you won may not be.

The first principle in making anything come about is to know what you want. Most of us think we know what we'd do if we came into a lot of money but really we don't have a clue beyond 'pay off my mortgage' and 'go on holiday'. Fine, but then what? Think properly about what you'd do if money were no object. I once spoke to a London cabbie about this and I really agreed with what he said. 'I don't understand people who go back to their normal work place when they've won a lot of money,' he said. 'It shows a lack of imagination. I mean, if I had a lot of money, I'd be in the Med, painting on a beach.' Like many of our fantastic cabbies, the man was a philosopher and he'd thought long and hard about what would make him happy. He knew because he'd already been for a short holiday to play out his millionaire lifestyle and so he knew what his ultimate goal was. I have no doubt that when he retires, you'll find him on the Med, painting on a beach.

Here's an idea for you...

Save up and visit a spa. A pampering visit to a place that smells nice and is geared toward your relaxation and enjoyment makes you feel like a million pounds sterling. If a spa isn't your scene then perhaps a round of golf somewhere? The point is that if you save up you can sometimes enjoy the same pleasures as the very rich and that will make you realise that the experience and not the bank balance is what really matters.

Wealth is not about money. Wealth is about how much you love life and lead it to the full. I noticed, during a time that I had very little money, that a free trip to the park was as exciting for my niece and nephew as the expensive outings I used to give them when I had money. It wasn't the pricey shows they were craving, it was my time and attention. So don't concentrate on the money when you think about what your perfect 'lottery life' would be like.

Most people have responsibilities that they'd take care of first like debts to be repaid and homes to buy. Then there's the helping of less fortunate members of the family and of friends. Then there are the holidays and fun times. However, what you need to figure out is what you'd do after the initial excitement had worn down. Would you return to your usual job? If so, you're very lucky as that means you do actually enjoy doing your job so much that you'd do it even if you didn't have to. Would you set up your own business? Or would you not work and live off the interest? If so, where would you live? How would you spend your day? Write out an itinerary of your perfect day, post-winning the lottery. Do you live by a beach; would you go for an early morning beach run? Who would you meet for lunch? At which restaurant?

Daydreaming about a perfect life where money's no object is an enjoyable way to learn about yourself and what it is that you want out of life. You may surprise yourself. You may think you're a bit of a homebody but then you discover that you'd travel continuously if you could, in which case adventure is more important to you. Compare your choices with that of your spouse and see if you both agree. It can lead to some interesting discussions. In the case of one couple I know, it was such an exciting prospect that they sold their urban flat and moved to Cornwall to start living in the way they said they wanted to when thinking about their lottery lives. This idea can change your life, if you really put your heart and soul into it. You see, money isn't always what's holding you back, fear of taking a risk often is. Go wild and become one of life's millionaires.

'Be as you wish to seem.'
SOCRATES, Greek philosopher

Defining idea...

213

How did
it go?

Q   **How can I think clearly about what my life would be like if I haven't any money to speak of? Isn't it a futile exercise?**

A   *No, that's just negative thinking. If you have already decided that you're never going to have your dreams come true so why bother dreaming at all, you've lost the battle before you've begun. Something that doesn't have immediate results is not futile, it's just that the usefulness is not on the surface but underneath in the sub-conscious bits of your mind. You're planting a seed so feed it, nurture it and don't drown it by raining heavily upon it before it's had a chance to germinate.*

Q   **I was doing this idea with my husband and it turns out our lottery lives are completely at odds – should I be worried?**

A   *Only if you win the lottery. You shouldn't be too worried as this is a thinking exercise, not a practical one so save the discussion for when you do actually have to decide on where to buy your home and how to live your life. Having differences in your lottery lives is only to be expected as you are individuals and won't agree on everything. You should only start worrying when your values are at odds; for example, if he decides that he wouldn't give a penny to help anyone else and you'd have family you'd want to help out. That is indicative of a possible difference in values.*

49

Silent, not sullen

Why silence can be a healing way towards inner peace. Sometimes the less said, the better.

Silence is golden because gold is a precious, desired commodity and so is silence. Value your store of it.

From the second you open your eyes in the morning, noise of all sorts assaults you. This isn't just aural noise but also visual noise, a riot of electronics, colours, voices; a veritable cacophony of 'stuff'. Dogs barking outside, traffic noise, gulls and building work all contribute to a tense, noisy atmosphere. How do we escape it? Well, if you're like most people, we escape the noise by piling more noise on.

We never really just sit and enjoy silence because it feels wasteful in modern life. It seems like we should fill every second with productivity, be it a call to a friend, organising your weekend plans, watching TV or listening to the radio. This 'noise' is something that we create ourselves and so we have more time for it. Besides, how uncomfortable do you get when you don't have all that noise going on around you?

Here's an idea for you...

Do a sponsored silence for one evening with your partner (get your kids involved if they're not too young). You can either have it be sponsored for charity or you can each sponsor the other £20 to buy something you fancy as a reward. Instead of stopping the silence if you accidentally say something, just add a pound for every word uttered. Try to do interesting things remaining silent, like a silent seduction or a silent game of chess with pre-agreed hand signals to indicate 'check', etc.

When was the last time you just sat in silence? We don't really do that because it seems slightly sad or depressing but this is the great myth of our time. Silence is not sad, needing noise is sad. You don't need a TV or a radio to keep you company, you have yourself. Plus there's a secret about silence that not many people know because not many people practise it.

Silence is the only time that you can hear yourself speak. Sound weird? Well, it is sort of but if you're looking for some guidance in what to do with your life or a situation, silence can provide the space to find some answers. That's why you don't hear about death metal meditation. It all tends to be silent meditation because that's when you're still and quiet enough for spirit to give you some pointers.

I went on a silence retreat once and the first couple of days were excruciating. I wanted to talk to people. I wanted to ask the monks who ran the retreat what made them decide to become monks and how long they had stayed silent for and do they ever go stir-crazy but I wasn't allowed to. The hardest thing was when I accidentally bumped into somebody and went 'sorry' and then 'sorry' for having said sorry. The person in question just smiled but I felt like I'd broken a fast or something.

A loving silence often has far more power to heal and to connect than the most well-intentioned words.

RACHEL NAOMI REMEN M.D.,
medical reformer, educator and
author

Defining idea...

By about the third day I noticed that every-thing had changed. My movements were more graceful and the constant voice in my head had stopped chattering on so incessantly. It was still there but it was much more likely to notice a rose in bloom than to wonder whether I'd left the gas on and whether my ex was dating anyone now etc., etc. I returned from the retreat more rested than I have been in years.

You don't have to go as drastic as a full-on retreat to enjoy silence. The next time you have the house to yourself, try lighting a candle and sitting in a comfortable position, looking into the flame. Let any noise from outside wash over you. You can notice it but don't attach yourself to it. It will feel strange at first, especially if you usually leap to turn on the TV when you have the house to yourself but it is well worth doing for a bit of calm contemplation.

How did it go?

Q   Are you meant to feel frustrated and restricted when you try to stay silent?

A   Yes! The first few times I did it, as a bit of a chatterbox, I felt very frustrated. Even when by myself, I wanted to sing and shout and break the silence but after a while, I noticed that even silence has different qualities and you only notice when you've been quiet a while. Persevere and you'll soon understand what the attraction is.

Q   I live in a really busy household and silence is impossible. What do you suggest?

A   How about finding a bolt-hole, perhaps a garden shed or the garden or even the cellar or attic? Make yourself a small space that you can call your own and then get a bit of silence there. Alternatively, get your silence fix in the bath. Put your ears under the water, now that's a very interesting sort of silence.

Q   Whenever we argue, my husband gives me the silent treatment. Surely that's not conducive to inner peace?

A   No, it isn't but I bet the silent treatment bugs you a whole lot more than an outright fight? Try to use it as an opportunity to disengage from the row and you try a bit of silence yourself. I recommend one of you breaks the silence eventually though as otherwise you'll forget what you were rowing about! A friend of mine does silly dances in front of her husband when he's not talking to her. Eventually he has to crack a smile, no matter how annoyed he is. Then they talk it out.

50

Fall in love with yourself

Self-love won't make you blind.

Loving yourself is a basic to any good human endeavour so the sooner you start, the sooner you'll see some wonderful results in your life.

When you catch a look at yourself in a mirror, do you say 'Wow, what bright eyes I have, they look great,' or do you focus on a double chin or blemished skin? Most people do the latter because we aren't really encouraged to think lovely thoughts about ourselves all the time. In fact this is actively discouraged as being a sign of vanity. While no-one wants the world to be full of vain people, it is true that so many problems like crime and abuse wouldn't arise if people didn't hate themselves so much. If you think the worst of yourself, you're capable of the worst. Opposite thought patterns yield opposite results.

Even if you think you're pretty nice to yourself, pay attention for a day to everything you say about yourself. For example, when someone gives you a compliment, do you deny what they're saying as quickly as possible? Do you discuss your failings

Here's an idea for you...

Kiss yourself in the mirror. You will definitely want to laugh and you'll be embarrassed as all hell if anyone catches you but it is a good way of realising how much we're averse to the idea of loving ourselves. A kiss is the ultimate gesture of acceptance and desire and yet it is something we can't offer ourselves without a great big hubbub. Be brave, kiss yourself passionately.

with your friends more than your successes? Pay close attention and then promise yourself a 'be nice to me' (BNTM) day. On your BNTM day don't allow anyone – especially not yourself – to say a word against you. Imagine that you're looking after a precious, vulnerable child and you have to protect her from anyone saying bad things to her. Take your task seriously and don't even allow passing thoughts of 'Doh, I'm so stupid' to enter your head. Try and think 'whoopsy' if you do something wrong. Once the day is over, decide whether you need to do it again. If it was fairly easy, then move on to the next exercise. If you found it hard, do it once a week until it becomes second nature. You're aiming to always stop yourself saying anything untoward about you or your abilities.

The next exercise to do is to get a pen and some lovely paper – the sort you'd use to write a romantic love letter on. Then write a letter to yourself as a child, writing down all the things you really loved about yourself. If you loved the fact that you stood up for younger kids in the playground or that time you made that painting that won a prize or that you were kind to your neighbour, write it down. Don't allow your letter to become 'balanced'. We don't want to hear in this particular letter about the time you smacked John Cottingley so hard he lost a tooth. Or about stealing that fiver from your nan's purse. Don't write down anything that makes you feel ashamed or upset but do write down how you have a strong sense of conscience that let you know the difference between right and wrong.

'You cannot be lonely if you like the person you're alone with.'
WAYNE W. DYER, self-help author

Defining idea...

Having written your letter (and I hope it's long), put it in an envelope, tie a pretty ribbon around it and put it in a special place with other mementoes. Then, whenever you have a day that you're feeling down and rotten, take out your letter and read about what a wonderful person you were, right from the very start.

Another way to express your love for yourself is to always get dressed properly in the morning and put your make-up on. This is even if your day just consists of sitting at home sending out CVs. Look as smart and well-dressed as you can afford because you should realise that you're not just dressing for other people but you're also dressing for the most important person in your life – you. This is one the first things that slips when people fall into depression. My mother always knows when I'm down because I don't wear make-up and she always nags me to put some slap on in order to feel more 'like myself' again. It also helps me like myself so I suppose there's something in it.

How did it go?

Q   How can I accept compliments gracefully?

A   *Smile, say 'thank you'. It's the simplest way to accept a compliment. Don't allow yourself to ruin it with a big explanation about how really you're usually quite hideous but you had your make-up done professionally today etc., etc.*

Q   Isn't self-love selfish love?

A   *Nope because we weren't given a finite quota of love when we were born. This means you're not depriving anyone of love by loving yourself. In fact the more you love yourself, the more capable you are of giving high-quality love to others. People with low self-esteem rarely know how to make others feel good either.*

Q   My boyfriend makes me feel terrible about myself. Should I split up with him?

A   *What do you think? You say yourself that he makes you feel terrible about yourself. Imagine for a minute that he was dating someone you really care about, like your sister or your mum. Would you allow anyone to treat your family or friends the way he treats you? If not, then you have your answer. Why should you be treated any worse than anyone else you care about? If you feel that the relationship can be salvaged, have an open and frank discussion about him, highlighting what he says and does to make you feel bad about yourself. Then see if he's prepared to change that behaviour. If he truly cares about you, he will be willing to change.*

51

It's not easy being green

Peas are green. So is peace.

Green living is not just something that fashionable young things do to get street cred — this is an issue for us all.

Loving our environment is something that seems to be intuitively right – you don't need a former Vice-President of one of the most shockingly un-green countries on the planet to tell you that. You can feel it just by sticking your head out of your car in rush hour traffic. You'll be choking and spluttering in the space of a few minutes and so is the planet. If I ruled the world, cars would be banned. Jeremy Clarkson would be a term of abuse. 'Oh you big Jeremy Clarkson!' kids would yell in the playground whenever someone let in an own goal. Then they'd get told off by their parents for using obscenities. Any man who positively encourages us to buy more and more gas-guzzling leviathan cars deserves to have his name turned into a swear word.

In cities there is absolutely no call for cars. Use the brilliant public transport systems we have. Oops. Forgot, sorry. The public transport system is a bit creaky at times and it does get regularly, in fact on a daily basis, shocked that loads of people want

Here's an idea for you...

Join greenmetropolis.com – this is the best idea I've come across in ages. You read a paperback, you then enter its ISBN on the site and they sell it for £3.75, giving you three quid and deducting their fee of 75p. You get an email telling you where to send the book second class. You're probably only making about £2 on each book, when you consider postage, but it's much better than clogging up your home with books you won't ever read again.

to use it during commuter rush hours. This seems to be the exact time that signals fail or some passenger decides to dive under the train in order for them to announce that a 'passenger action' has caused the delay. This sounds almost accusatory as if to say 'Yes, we know that 99% of the time the delays are our fault but this one is one of you lot actually so don't moan at us'. So public transport sucks but the more you use it, the more people there are who can campaign to have it made good and efficient.

While the companies running our public transport sort themselves out you can help by car pooling. Send an email around the office and find out if some of your colleagues live near you. Then share petrol and a ride in together. This will save the planet much of the aforementioned choking. Get your company to introduce a recycling scheme for paper and plastics. There are several awards out there given to companies who introduce green and ethical practices into their businesses. Convince your boss that a shiny new plaque saying how great the company is at saving the planet will be a real draw for customers and suppliers alike.

Remember small things like not leaving TVs and computers on standby and turning off the tap when you brush your teeth. Switching to energy-saving lightbulbs, insulating your loft and installing double-glazing are all ways that you'll not only save energy but also save on your bills. A double win.

'Whatever befalls the earth, befalls the people of the earth. Man did not weave the web of life; he is merely a strand in it.'
CHIEF SEATTLE, Native American leader

Defining idea…

Limit the amount of long-haul journeys you make and always off-set your carbon footprint by purchasing some trees to be planted somewhere suitable. Bear in mind that it's pointless signing up to a pine tree type scheme that some cheeky so-and-sos are passing off as good carbon off-setting schemes. What you need is someone who is planting native trees and retaining bio-diversity. Pine trees are the junk food giants of the carbon neutral movement. Check out a scheme like the Earth C.O.S.T. programme or see if there's a scheme in your local area.

Above all, as you make greener and greener choices, you must remember not to get smug. Nobody likes a smug environmentalist. No earnestness either, please. Just do your bit and try to convince those in your sphere of influence to do their bits but don't start a witch hunt to see which of your mates forgets to wash out yoghurt cartons and put them in the recycling box. That's a surefire way to get your friends muttering about what a right Jeremy Clarkson you are.

How did it go?

Q **We don't have a recycling scheme in my neighbourhood and I don't drive so I can't go to the recycling point in town. How do I make a difference?**

A   *Write to your local council and find out why they don't have a scheme in your area. If they aren't able to give you a satisfactory answer, think about getting a petition together with your neighbours to show the authorities that there is support for a recycling scheme.*

Q **Isn't climate change a myth?**

A   *Tut, tut, tut, to the back of the class with you. You're acting like the senator in disaster movies who says to the maverick scientist that there is no problem and then gets washed away by a tidal wave. You don't want to be washed away by a tidal wave, do you? Well then, get with the programme.*

Q **Will I have to start eating tofu if I get involved with green projects?**

A   *Ah, you've named one of my chief fears. While it is true that there are a high proportion of vegetarians in environmentalist circles, it's not necessary to become one just because you want to help save the planet. I would say, though, that any meat or fish you eat should be in the right season and from a sustainable, local source. When you buy produce out of season in a supermarket, you're paying for the air miles it took to transport it there. Bad for the environment and not particularly tasty either.*

52

Travel broadens your hips

While travelling has much to recommend it, inner peace requires a hearth and home.

Do you remember that programme
The Littlest Hobo? It was about a
wandering dog that helped people out
and then hit the road after his good work was
done.

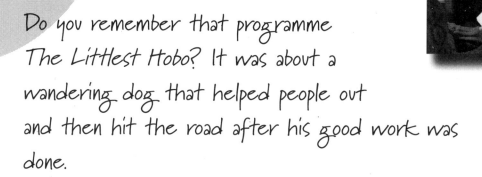

While that dog may have had very good reasons for his constant wanderings (chiefly a lucrative TV series contract since there's not much of a programme to be made out of 'and then they lived happily ever after'), we should not emulate his example. We're not the stars of TV shows and, even if we are, we all need a place to call 'home'.

Your home has a spirit. No, stop freaking out; not a ghost, a spirit. You can usually feel that spirit best in the first moment that you arrive back home. Does the house feel heavy or light; welcoming or lonely; happy or sad? You can sometimes palpably

Here's an idea for you...

Build a literal hearth in your home. This can be a real fire if you're lucky enough to have one, or a gas one if you can afford one. Alternatively it can be as simple as getting a bunch of sturdy pillar candles and lighting them grouped together in a suitably fire-safe place. Basically you're creating a place to sit with your loved ones in the evening and look into a naked flame. There's nothing better or more peaceful.

feel heaviness in the atmosphere of a place after a row has taken place there. There is energy within a home that can be affected by what happens to it and within it.

Today, take a walk around your home looking for energy blockages or problems. This could be a very practical thing like a broken door handle or it could be a more spiritual thing like a corner that feels dark and depressing while other parts of the room are fine. Make a list of everything, no matter how small, that's amiss. Then set yourself a tiny target; fix one thing each weekend. Don't give yourself any more than one thing as an aim as otherwise you'll feel overwhelmed. If, once you've done that one thing, you want to do something else, feel free, but you're not obliged to. When irritations such as the drawer that jams or the spotlight in the bathroom that needs changing are removed, you'll feel the energy lift and change. It will be as if things are flowing better.

On the 'dark, depressing corners' problem, a very popular way of dealing with this in the Native American (and hippy-trippy) cultures is to smudge. This involves burning a bundle of sage, considered a cleansing herb, putting it out so that it is smoking and then wafting that aromatic smoke through each of the rooms of your home. It is good to work clockwise around each room, ensuring the smoke goes into every corner. The cat will look at you as if you're barmy but I've found it works brilliantly at making your home energetically squeaky clean.

Once you've fixed all your odd jobs and energetically cleansed your home, start walking around and thinking about it cosmetically. Does your home represent who you are now or is it a reflection of you in your student days, or indeed is it primarily filled with your boyfriend's things if you moved in with him? Have a family meeting with all the occupants of your house and make some joint decisions about how to improve the décor and condition of your home. Think about bright new colours and don't be afraid to repaint furniture (as long as it isn't an antique!).

This redecorating doesn't need to cost an arm and a leg – think creatively. If your sofa is a bit tired but you can't afford a new one, get a nice patterned throwover to put over it. If you can't afford a new kitchen, see if you can afford changing just the cabinet handles for a cheaper way to freshen up the look. Most of all, show your home you love it by keeping it as clean and tidy as you can.

'Nor need we power or splendour, wide hall or lordly dome; the good, the true, the tender, these form the wealth of home.'
SARAH J. HALE, author

Defining idea…

How did it go?

Q **I really hate my home, it's in a bad part of town and it's pretty dank and miserable but I can't afford to move. How can I improve it?**

A *Your home will never be lovely if you don't love it. It may scrub up OK but you have to love it for it to be really charming. Stop saying you hate it, try some cosmetic fixes like some painting and maybe new curtains and start showering time and affection on your home. It will pay you back by being a lot more lovable.*

Q **I have the neighbour from hell and home is not a pleasant place to be any more – what should I do?**

A *I completely sympathise. We once had to move house because of a violent and unreasonable neighbour (it later transpired she had a mental illness and so couldn't help her behaviour). It is intolerable when your home life is wrecked by outside influences like that. Try imagining a golden bubble of protection around your home whenever you sit in meditation. See if this works. If it doesn't, I'm afraid that moving may be on the cards.*

Q **My flatmate is always at home. How do I get some solitary space?**

A *I'm assuming your flatmate works so perhaps you might want to book a day off from your work and just spend it at home? If you like it, you could even spend a week's holiday at home instead of jetting off abroad and that will afford you lots of me-time during the day.*

The end...

Or is it a new beginning?

We hope that these ideas will have inspired you to try new things to feed your soul. We hope you've found the benefit in nurturing your inner self and used these great ideas to take your focus away from the material and develop your spiritual side. You should be well on your way to a more relaxed and sorted you.

So why not let us know about it? Tell us how you got on. What did it for you – what really helped you bring calm into your hectic life? Maybe you've got some tips of your own that you'd like to share. If you liked this you may find we have more brilliant ideas for other areas that could help change your life for the better. You'll find us, and a host of other brilliant ideas, online at www.infideas.com.

Or if you prefer to write, then send your letters to:
The brilliant book of calm
Infinite Ideas Ltd
36 St Giles, Oxford, OX1 3LD, United Kingdom

We want to know what you think, because we're all working on making our lives better too. Give us your feedback and you could win a copy of another *52 Brilliant Ideas* book of your choice. Or maybe get a crack at writing your own.

Good luck. Be brilliant.

Offer one

CASH IN YOUR IDEAS

We hope you enjoy this book. We hope it inspires, amuses, educates and entertains you. But we don't assume that you're a novice, or that this is the first book that you've bought on the subject. You've got ideas of your own. Maybe our author has missed an idea that you use successfully. If so, why not put it in an email and send it to: yourauthormissedatrick@infideas.com, and if we like it we'll post it on our bulletin board. Better still, if your idea makes it into print we'll send you four books of your choice or the cash equivalent. You'll be fully credited so that everyone knows you've had another Brilliant Idea.

Offer two

HOW COULD YOU REFUSE?

Amazing discounts on bulk quantities of Infinite Ideas books are available to corporations, professional associations and other organisations.

For details call us on:
+44 (0)1865 514888
fax: +44 (0)1865 514777
or e-mail: info@infideas.com

Where it's at ...